I.M. GREENGARTEN received his PhD from the University of Toronto and works as an administrator in geriatric care in Toronto.

Thomas Hill Green (1836-1882) was a leading British philosopher and political figure and founder of the school of British Idealism, which displaced the philosophy of Bentham and John Stuart Mill as the dominant tradition in British universities from 1880 into the twentieth century.

Greengarten presents a detailed analysis of Green's thought, including his theories of political obligation, property, self-realization, and human nature, and develops the necessary tools for an analysis of Green's work and the tradition of liberal-democratic thought.

He finds in Green a view of human nature and human potentialities which is in striking contrast to the views of earlier liberal thinkers, and remarkably similar to that of Marx – despite Green's clear and often passionate defence of capitalism and market freedom. His concept of human nature is of a divided, self-contradictory nature; his theory of the true good is of a good that is to be shared, a common good that is not attainable through the selfish pursuit of private goods; his vision of the good society foresees the elimination of class-based conflict and inequality.

Greengarten examines Green's proposals for legislative reform and the goals to which they would lead – the elimination of poverty, and the establishment of a classless society wherein all members would have equal opportunity to develop and realize their potential.

This book offers a fresh perspective on Green and raises issues of importance in the field of social and political theory.

I.M. GREENGARTEN

Thomas Hill Green and the Development of Liberal-Democratic Thought

UNIVERSITY OF TORONTO PRESS
Toronto Buffalo London

© University of Toronto Press 1981
Toronto Buffalo London
Reprinted in paperback 2017

ISBN 978-0-8020-5503-3 (cloth)
ISBN 978-1-4875-9927-0 (paper)

Canadian Cataloguing in Publication Data

Greengarten, I.M., 1949-
Thomas Hill Green and the development of
liberal-democratic thought
Includes index.
ISBN 978-0-8020-5503-3 (bound)   ISBN 978-1-4875-9927-0 (pbk.)
1. Green, Thomas Hill, 1836-1882 – Political Science.
I. Title.
BI637.G74   192   C80-094653-7

This book has been published with the help of grants from the Social Science Federation of
Canada, using funds provided by the Social Sciences and Humanities Research Council of
Canada, and from the Publications Fund of University of Toronto Press.

To Ena

Contents

Preface

This book began as a study of both Thomas Hill Green and John Stuart Mill: Green because the major assumptions and inconsistencies of liberal-democratic thought are clearer in his work than in that of any other early writer of this tradition; Mill because he is unquestionably the most important and best known of the liberal-democratic thinkers. Limitations of time and the pressures of other responsibilities prevented me from finishing my task.

The study of Green is complete. Whatever the strengths and weaknesses of Green's work – and there are a good number of entries on both sides of the ledger – I hope these are elucidated here. However, as a teacher who captivated his large student audiences, as a scholar who changed the course of philosophical thought in British universities for decades, and as a politician/theoretician who influenced the policies of British governments, Green has received far too little attention from political theorists of all persuasions. I believe this study goes some way towards correcting that imbalance.

The examination of Mill is only at its beginning; I look forward to a time when it too might be completed. To begin with Green, however, was essential. The significant elements of the liberal-democratic world-view are unmistakably present in Mill's thought, but they are not easily uncovered. They are obscured largely by the baggage of utilitarianism he felt compelled to carry. In attempting to straddle the two traditions – the liberal and the liberal-democratic – Mill did full justice to neither. Green, who was under no such philosophical restriction, was able to embrace with far less reservation the ideas of the new age. To Green's aforementioned accomplishments should be added, in my view, the fact that he is the key to unlocking the complexities of Mill's thought.

The appendix comparing Mill and Green is based on the rather extensive research I have compiled towards the final study. I have chosen to include this chapter because I feel it underscores a point I very much want to make. The concepts and tools of analysis I have developed or applied in examining Green can and should be applied to Mill and, indeed, to the whole liberal-democratic tradition from Mill to the present. It follows that they are indispensable to a full understanding of the modern welfare state.

Many individuals helped bring this project to fruition. I wish to acknowledge in particular the assistance of C.B. Macpherson. His concern, questioning, and guidance were invaluable to me in preparing this study. The scholarly debt which I owe him will be obvious to the reader; his ideas form a large part of the foundation upon which I have endeavoured to build my critique of liberal-democratic thought. I wish to express my gratitude as well to A.A. Kontos and R.A. Fenn of the Department of Political Economy, University of Toronto, for their thoughtful and incisive criticism, not to mention their much-needed moral support. To all of my friends and colleagues who read or commented on all or part of the manuscript go my sincere thanks.

Finally, I wish to thank my wife, Ena, to whom I have dedicated this book. She was always available to help sort out my ideas, always ready to help me over the inevitable and countless stumbling-blocks, always there with a word of support and encouragement when I needed it most. In short, without her, this book would not have seen the light of day.

Abbreviations

When not cited in full, references to Green's works are given as follows:

Works   *Works of Thomas Hill Green.* Three volumes. Edited by R.L.
                   Nettleship. New York: AMS Press, 1973. Reprint of 1911-18 ed.
                   published by Longmans, Green, London. Volume number is
                   indicated simply by I, II, or III.
Hume I   *Introductions to Hume's 'Treatise of Human Nature': I. General
                   Introduction. Works,* I
Hume II   *Introductions to Hume's 'Treatise of Human Nature': II. Introduc-
                   tion to the Moral Part of Hume's 'Treatise.' Works,* I
Lectures on Kant *Lectures on the Philosophy of Kant: I. The 'Critique of Pure
                   Reason'* and *II. The Metaphysics of Ethics. Works,* II
Lectures on Logic *Lectures on Logic: I. The Logic of the Formal Logicians* and *II. The
                   Logic of J.S. Mill. Works,* II
PE   *Prolegomena to Ethics.* Edited by A.C. Bradley. New York:
                   Thomas Y. Crowell, 1969
PPO   *Lectures on the Principles of Political Obligation. Works,* II
Spencer & Lewes *Mr. Herbert Spencer and Mr. G.H. Lewes: Their Application of the
                   Doctrine of Evolution to Thought. Works,* I

THOMAS HILL GREEN AND THE DEVELOPMENT
OF LIBERAL-DEMOCRATIC THOUGHT

I

Introduction: an unsettled and unsettling age

The rise of industrial capitalism in the last half of the eighteenth century was to have a profound revolutionary impact on the social, economic, and political life of nineteenth-century England. A period of unparalleled prosperity and progress for the few, it was an era of hardship, starvation, and economic depression for the many. Although the technology that might liberate humankind from scarcity and deprivation had at last been developed, the contradictions and inequities of the market system were becoming more and more manifest.

The royal commission reports of this period recount the human suffering in minute detail. The dangerous and debilitating working conditions in the factories, the overcrowded and unhealthy living conditions of the slums of great cities, the child labour, the starvation, and the misery are all duly and faithfully recorded. At the same time the poverty and insecurity of the working class were aggravated by the periodic economic crises of the century: the crisis of the thirties and early forties, the commercial collapse of the fifties, and the Great Depression of 1873-96.

Conditions such as these gave birth to the British trade union movement. Despite the punitive Combination Laws of 1799 and 1800 and the repeated attempts to destroy the union movement even after their repeal in 1824, trade union activity and membership increased. Fired by revolutionary movements on the continent – the mid-century uprisings no less than the Paris Commune of 1871 – pressure for economic reform grew, especially during the first half of the century, and was joined by demands for political reform, represented most notably by the Chartist Movement. Meanwhile, throughout this period, Irish resistance to the government at Westminster continued to grow as the wounds created by British economic and political domination of Ireland were allowed to fester.

It is in light of this situation that the reforming legislation of the last century must be understood. The spreading industrialization and the continued development of the market economy were creating a more and more restive, more and more dangerous working class, without at the same time providing any institutionalized means of insulating its members from the system's inevitable shocks and inequities. The political reforms of 1832, 1867, and 1884-5; the health and housing legislation of 1858 and 1875; the Education Acts of 1870, 1876, and 1880; and, most significant of all, the various Factory Acts, regulating conditions in the work-place and hours of employment, of 1802, 1833, 1837, 1844, 1848, 1850, 1867, 1872, 1875, 1878, and 1880; these reforms were introduced primarily to meet the threat to the whole edifice of capitalism posed by the rising tide of discontent.

It was into this unsettled and unsettling age that Thomas Hill Green was born in 1836, son of the rector of Birkin, Yorkshire, and the youngest of four children. Educated at Rugby from 1850 to 1855, he entered Balliol College in October 1855, where he remained as student and teacher until his early death in 1882. During his many years at the university, Green lived a fairly active political life. In 1865-6 he served as an assistant commissioner to the Schools Inquiry Commission. After his marriage in 1871 to Charlotte Symonds he became involved with the English temperance movement, serving in a number of official capacities. In 1874 he was elected, on his second attempt, to the Oxford School Board, established in 1871, and in 1876 he was elected to the Oxford Town Council representing the North Ward.[1]

A number of writers have maintained that a major aim of Green's work was to justify and defend the reform legislation of the nineteenth century.[2] To a limited extent this thesis is essentially correct. In Green's view the physical and moral degradation of the lower class lay as a heavy burden on society as a whole. No member of society could achieve a truly moral existence while other members were prevented from doing so. Accordingly, he saw social legislation as the means by which the lower class could be moralized.[3] Although the currently dominant philosophy, utilitarianism, demanded, and was in practice largely responsible for, such

1 R.L. Nettleship, 'Memoir,' in *Works*, III, pp. xi, xii, xvi, xlv, cviii, cxiv, cxv, cxviii, clx
2 See, for example, Sir Ernest Barker, *Political Thought in England: 1848 to 1914*, 2d ed. (London: Oxford University Press, 1947), p. 22; Y.L. Chin, *The Political Theory of Thomas Hill Green*, PHD dissertation (New York: W.D. Gray, 1920), p. 97; A.D. Lindsay, 'T.H. Green and the Idealists,' in F.J.C. Hearnshaw, ed., *The Social and Political Ideas of Some Representative Thinkers of the Victorian Age* (New York: Barnes and Noble, 1933), p. 163; and Melvin Richter, *The Politics of Conscience: T.H. Green and his Age* (London: Weidenfeld and Nicolson, 1964), pp. 204 and 283.
3 Through legislation, Green hoped to transform the proletariat into capitalists, and thereby to create a classless society – classless in the shared consciousness of its members, not in the distribution of wealth or capital.

legislation, Green argued that theoretically it had no logical basis for making such demands: 'the modern English utilitarian is generally better than his logic.'[4]

However, to appreciate fully the value as well as the limitations of Green's social and political philosophy, one must be aware that it represented much more than this. It was to the major questions of his time that Green addressed himself, and the most serious of these in his view was that his society was internally threatened, from below by the growing demand for political and economic equality and from above by complacency and an unwillingness to compromise. England was on the verge of ruin, and utilitarianism and the empirical psychology on which it was founded were failing to provide the direction necessary to avert the impending catastrophe. If a long-term remedy were to be found, a new set of principles was required: 'man, above all modern man, must theorize his practice, and the failure adequately to do so, must cripple the practice itself.'[5] The solution, he believed, lay in a fundamental restructuring of English philosophy: in a re-examination of the foundations of society and political obligation and in a redefinition of the very ends of human endeavour. Convinced that this task could not be accomplished within the framework of the dominant philosophical system of his day, a point he sought to establish incontrovertibly in his painstaking analysis of the principal exponents of the empirical tradition,[6] Green turned to Kant and Hegel.

It was in German Idealism that Green found the theoretical tools he needed to execute his plan. From Kant and Hegel he learned to look beyond the immediate data of experience, to see in them a purpose, a grand scheme, which the spiritual heirs of Locke and Hume had failed to discern. He learned, moreover, to distinguish the appearance of things – and persons – from their true nature, to see in human desires and activity not simply the blind play of natural forces but the struggle to realize an ideal essence. Above all, he discovered that man is capable of change, of improvement, and that his social, economic, and political institutions must be designed accordingly.

As we shall see, Green's ambitious venture was to fail, as did John Stuart Mill's attempted restatement of utilitarianism, undertaken for much the same reason, because he himself failed to perceive the true nature of the dilemma that confronted his society.[7] While he succeeded in injecting a new democratic principle into the liberal philosophic framework of capitalism, Green yet remained faithful to the pos-

---

4 'Popular Philosophy in its Relation to Life,' *Works*, III, p. 124.
5 Ibid.
6 See especially Green's critique of Locke and Hume (as well as Berkeley), in *Hume I* and *Hume II*.
7 Green and Mill are compared in the appendix below.

sessive individualism upon which that system rests.[8] The true dilemma of his society was the dilemma of industrial capitalism; the inequities, the contradictions, the degradation, and the demoralization were the result, not of the inability of men to cope with these problems, but of the failure of the system itself, its inherent inability to produce any long-term solutions to those problems. In remaining consistent with the market ethos – personal independence, private property in one's goods and person, the right of unlimited individual appropriation – Green incorporated into his model of the good society and the truly moral man those very elements which formed the underlying cause of the crisis of his age. In this sense, then, Green's work is justificatory, not merely of the social legislation of nineteenth-century England, but of the capitalist market system itself.

2

This line of argument has been implicitly challenged by Melvin Richter in his influential study of Green.[9] His thesis is that Green's work should be understood as primarily a reaction to the religious climate of his time, 'the great crisis of faith precipitated by science and scholarship.'[10] According to Richter, religion was being attacked, on the one hand by science, especially the theory of evolution, and on the other hand by the higher criticism of the Bible, both of which were eroding the traditional basis of Christian belief, namely, dogma and proof by miracle. 'To most mid-Victorians, it seemed that men were forced to choose between faith and reason.'[11] Green, in this view, 'thought that he could remove the ostensible conflict between the truths of science and the truths of religion; that he could provide through his philosophy an unassailable foundation for belief.'[12]

There can be no doubt that religion played a central role in Green's life and work. Raised in a religious family, Green expressed an intense interest in matters related

8 See C.B. Macpherson, *The Political Theory of Possessive Individualism: Hobbes to Locke* (Oxford: at the Clarendon Press, 1962).
9 *The Politics of Conscience* and his 'T.H. Green and his Audience: Liberalism as a Surrogate Faith,' *Review of Politics*, XVIII: No. 4 (Oct. 1956)
10 *The Politics of Conscience*, p. 15. Jean Pucelle also argues that Green's theology is the key to the understanding of his entire philosophy. See his *L'Idéalisme en Angleterre: De Coleridge à Bradley* (Neuchatel: Éditions de la Baconnière, 1955), Chapter 4; and *La Nature et l'Esprit dans la Philosophie de T.H. Green: La Renaissance de l'Idéalisme en Angleterre au XIXe siècle*, 2 vols (Paris and Louvain: Béatrice Nauwelaerts/Éditions Nauwelaerts, 1960 and 1965). See also, Paul Montagné, *Un Radical Religieux en Angleterre au XIXe Siècle ou la Philosophie de Thomas Hill Green* (Toulouse: Imprimerie Ouvrière, 1927).
11 *The Politics of Conscience*, p. 25
12 Ibid., p. 27, cf. pp. 106-7; and, John Dewey, 'The Philosophy of Thomas Hill Green,' *Andover Review*, XI: No. 64 (April 1889), p. 339

to Christianity, and even thought of becoming a Nonconformist preacher.[13] He wrote and spoke on theological questions throughout his career at Oxford.[14] As one might expect from a devoutly religious individual, God is given a prominent position in Green's metaphysics and his ethics, in the form of the divine Eternal Consciousness, the spiritual principle in man and nature. It is certain, too, that Green's 'Puritan connection'[15] had a part in the formation of his conception of human nature.[16]

To be sure, Richter's analysis of Green's theology is extremely valuable and insightful while remaining faithful to both textual and historical evidence. However, by interpreting Green's political thought as, at bottom, a function of his religious philosophy, he reduces it to little more than a civic religion.[17] Such a procedure obscures the essential context and meaning of Green's politics. That Green's religion made him more sensitive to certain of the problems of his time; that it contributed to his adoption of one among several possible solutions to these problems; that it led him to cloak his social and political philosophy in terminology more appropriate to theology; all of this may be fully and freely admitted without abandoning the argument that his thought reflects the social, political, and economic climate of nineteenth-century English society, and that one of its fundamental aims was to justify the industrial-capitalist basis of that society. Indeed, the definite political elements in Green's thought cannot be understood as aspects of a theology.

Moreover, in view of Green's early and continuing interest in social and political questions,[18] as well as his political activity, politics was at least as important an

13 James Bryce, 'Professor T.H. Green: In Memoriam,' *Contemporary Review*, XLI (May 1882), p. 880

14 Green's major theological writings were as follows: 'Christian Dogma' (1858), 'The Witness of God' (1870), and 'Faith' (1877), all in *Works*, III; and the unpublished 'Life and Immortality Brought to Light by the Gospel' (1860), referred to by Nettleship in his 'Memoir' as the 'Ellerton Essay' and reproduced in Jean Pucelle, *La Nature et l'Esprit dans la Philosophie de T.H. Green*, II, pp. 268-81. In addition, there are the Fragments on 'Immortality' (?) and 'The Word is Nigh Thee' (?), as well as his lectures on the New Testament, 'The Conversion of Paul,' 'Justification by Faith,' and 'The Incarnation,' all dating from the 1870s, and all in *Works*, III.

15 Richter, *The Politics of Conscience*, p. 40

16 Richter also suggests that Green's religion 'made it impossible for him to be either a clear-cut individualist or collectivist' (ibid., p. 24).

17 See for example ibid., pp. 19, 24, 30, 32, and 134. Green's 'thought undeniably was a political theology' (p. 210).

18 Regarding Green's days at Rugby, Nettleship writes: 'That he was one of the recognized "politicians" of the school, and that he was considered (in spite of his own protestations to the contrary) a "dreadful radical," we learn from his letters' ('Memoir,' *Works*, III, p. xiv). For further discussion of his political interest and activities, see ibid., pp. xx-xxv, xliv-xlv, lxi, cx-cxx, clx; John Addington Symonds, *The Letters of John Addington Symonds*, 3 vols, ed. Herbert M. Schueller and Robert L. Peters (Detroit: Wayne State University Press, 1968-9), II, p. 777; and W. Wallace, 'Prof. T.H. Green,' *The Academy*, New Issue, No. 517 (1 April 1882), p. 231.

influence in his life as religion, certainly in his later years. The number and extent of his writings dedicated to the consideration of social, political, and economic problems testifies to the significance he attached to such matters. If he did not consider such problems to be more important and more pressing for English society than the religious crisis of his time (and there is sufficient evidence that he did), he undoubtedly believed them to be no less so.[19]

More important, however, Richter misunderstands Green's intention. Although religion has a basic role to play in his world-view, it shares the stage with art and philosophy.[20] This tripartite theme runs throughout Green's writings, although the third element, philosophy, changes according to the context. In the earliest formulation of his theme he speaks 'of art, of religion and philosophy'[21]; elsewhere he refers to art, religion and, variously, 'the conception of freedom and right,' 'political life,' and 'morality.'[22] Green appears to have intended the term 'morality' to represent both theory and practice, in fact the unity of theory and practice, the activity of man as a moral agent, as reflected both in his contemplation of that agency, that is, in his social and political philosophy, and in its practical application, that is, in the social and political institutions he creates.[23]

According to Green it is in these three realms that man expresses his attempt to overcome his individuality; through art, religion, and philosophy (theory and practice) man seeks to transcend the individual limitations of the animal consciousness and existence with which he is burdened in order to attain the freedom of a universal spiritual existence.[24] It is this eternal quest, man's attempt to construct an ideal existence for himself, that Green endeavours to explain because, he feels, it cannot be satisfactorily explained by the accepted methods. 'Art, religion, and political life have outgrown the nominalistic logic and the psychology of individual introspection; yet the only recognized formulae by which the speculative man can account for them

19 It does not say much of the man or his work to argue that the main concern of someone so obviously interested in politics in such an uncertain and potentially volatile political environment should be a theological crisis.

20 This view is apparently a borrowed and modified version of the original Hegelian conception.

21 'An Estimate of the Value and Influence of Works of Fiction in Modern Times,' Works, III, p. 22; cf. p. 23, where he refers to 'speculative philosophy.'

22 'Popular Philosophy in its Relation to Life,' Works, III, pp. 117, 124; Lectures on Kant, sec. 68; cf. 'Popular Philosophy in its Relation to Life,' p. 122.

23 Green's writing on art is confined, by and large, to a treatment of poetry. His only work devoted entirely to the subject is his early 'An Estimate of the Value and Influence of Works of Fiction in Modern Times,' which gained the Chancellor's Prize in 1862 ('Memoir,' Works, III, p. xxx.) Further discussion of his philosophy of art is scattered: 'The Influence of Civilization on Genius' (?), Works, III, pp. 18-19; 'Popular Philosophy in its Relation to Life' (1868), Works, III, pp. 118-20; Lectures on Kant (1875-6 and 1878-9), sec. 68 n. 1, and sec. 81; 'Faith' (1877), Works, III, pp. 168-9; and, PE (1882), sec. 1.

24 'Popular Philosophy in its Relation to Life,' Works, III, p. 117

to himself, are derived from that logic and psychology.'[25] As we shall see, that view of man as a passive receiver of external impulses, which Green traces as far back as Locke and as far forward as Spencer, Lewes, and Henry Sidgwick, simply cannot account for such activity. 'If *man as an artist*, and *man as himself a hell or heaven*, practically contradicts the philosophy that would confine him within the dark chamber of passive sense, not less certainly, though in more familiar ways, does he do so *as a citizen*.'[26]

Philosophy nevertheless plays a dual role in Green's system. It serves not only as one of man's self-transcending activities but also as that activity by which alone man is able to explain to himself both his ideals, however they may be expressed, and his struggle to actualize them.[27] From that point of view Green undertook his critique of empiricism and, on the positive side, the statement of his own philosophy. His purpose was to develop a theory of human knowledge and desire that would imply a human nature capable of art, religion, and philosophy (theory and practice). Green's philosophy is not, as Richter would have us believe, an outgrowth and justification of his theology but rather the unifying element of a world-view in which religion, though significant, is by no means the basis of the entire structure.

Keeping the importance of religion in Green's life and work in mind, one may legitimately study his philosophy as an independent statement, that is, his conception of man's social and political activity in both its theoretical and practical aspects, from its foundation in his metaphysics, to its culmination in his theory of human nature and the good society. That such a study will also explain man's religious and artistic activity follows from Green's system.[28] Indeed, my contention is that only such a procedure can be consistent with Green's intentions and hence fully appreciative of his meaning; only that way can we understand not only his social and political thought but his work as a whole – the true unity of his thought.

3

The major impetus to Green's work should therefore be traced to the social, political, and economic problems of nineteenth-century England, which were threatening to destroy his society and way of life. Believing that utilitarianism and the tradition

---

25   Ibid., p. 124
26   Ibid., p. 122; emphasis added. Cf. *Hume II*, sec. 64, where Green refers to the saint, the patriot, and the poet.
27   PE, sec. I. Richter does not seem to have entirely understood this passage (*The Politics of Conscience*, p. 167).
28   It might even be convincingly argued, though I will not attempt to do so, that the religious crisis of his time was itself ultimately the result of social, political, and economic forces at work in Green's society.

on which it was based were unable either to show how to solve the immediate crisis or ultimately to provide a solid theoretical underpinning for a stable and secure society, Green set out to formulate a philosophy that could. His approach was to enunciate a new theory of human nature that could serve, in turn, as the basis for a new theory of political obligation, a new cement for a society coming apart at the seams. I shall attempt to demonstrate that Green's theory was built upon a possessive individualist foundation, modified by the new facts of an industrialized market society.

I shall argue further that, although Green failed to realize it, his theory of human nature is self-contradictory.[29] While he perceived the moral bankruptcy and ineffectiveness of 'the Hobbes-to-Bentham concept of man,'[30] he failed to purge his own theory completely of this concept. He endowed man with an insatiable appetite for material goods; at the same time he posited that man is essentially an exerter and realizer of his uniquely human capacities. I argue that this dual nature of man as conceived by Green is internally inconsistent, and I shall examine the basis of and reasons for it. An important aspect of this inconsistency is worth noting in light of the problems of England in Green's time. Whereas the fulfilment of the former aspect of human nature implies a capitalist market society, the complete and equal realization of the latter aspect is incompatible with such a society.

It is instructive that Green died in 1882, less than a year before Marx.[31] Both of them had analysed and tried to comprehend the same England. (Marx settled in

29 This thesis is based upon C.B. Macpherson's argument 'that the ontological assumptions of our Western democratic theory have been, for something like a hundred years, internally inconsistent, comprising as they do two concepts of the human essence which are in the circumstances incompatible. One of these is the liberal, individualist concept of man as essentially a consumer of utilities, an infinite desirer and infinite appropriator ... The other is the concept of man as an enjoyer and exerter of his uniquely human attributes or capacities.' *Democratic Theory: Essays in Retrieval* (Oxford: at the Clarendon Press, 1973), p. 24. For a full statement of this theory see Essays I, II, and III.

30 Ibid., p. 11

31 Although it cannot be said for certain whether Green was familiar with the works of Marx himself, he was aware of the movement with which Marx was associated. Five years after the establishment of the International Working Men's Association in London, Green writes: '"Culture" and the "International" present themselves to me as due to the same disease of modern life as the High-Church Revival. I don't mean by this either to put all three on a level, or to imply their condemnation. I regard the "Church" as having, in virtue of the ideas which it retains from the New Testament, a much higher and truer Gospel for the individual than either "Culture" or the "International": and when I speak of them as due to a disease, I quite admit that in a sense all human life is a disease, and that any system which is to do good to man must be adapted to the present stage of the disease. But no recognition of the good present effect of any mode of sentiment or discipline can reconcile one to it when one finds it resting on doctrines that seem untrue.' Letter to Henry Scott Holland, October 1869; in *Henry Scott Holland, Memoir and Letters*, ed. by Stephen Paget (London: John Murray, 1921), p. 42

London in 1849; Green's earliest essays of a political nature date to the late 1850s.) Moreover, the roots of both their systems may be traced to German Idealism, and both thinkers criticized severely, though upon different grounds, the classical liberal theory of human nature. Needless to say, their conclusions were poles apart.

The industrial market society of England in the last century was in fact equally apprehended in both systems; the thought of each man was equally an expression of the age. From this point of view, Green's philosophy assumes a significance not usually attached to it. I shall argue that Green's system, like Marx's, represents in its own way the new forces liberated by the industrial revolution, that Green's self-contradictory theory of human nature is a manifestation of the alienation Marx perceived in capitalist market society. Marx, in postulating the abolition of capitalism, gave voice to the enormous human and technological potentialities of the age; Green, in assuming the continued existence of market society, defined its inherent limitations.

2

Philosophical foundations

Green's epistemology forms the basis of his ethics as well as the foundation of his theory of human nature. In attempting to establish his theory upon unassailable ground Green, following the example of earlier social philosophers, began with what he believed to be the most elementary of human faculties, knowledge, or the process of coming to know the world. By examining this faculty, he thought he could demonstrate the existence of a spiritual principle in man as the condition of both his morality and his capacity for social life and political obligation. In fact his argument rested on a set of assumptions – including the notion of the existence of a spiritual principle – that remained unstated and could not be proved. As one writer has recently argued, he could have made his case just as well without his metaphysics, by simply developing his moral philosophy on explicit assumptions.[1]

Although this judgment is undoubtedly true, Green's procedure corresponded to the intellectual practice of the philosophical community he was addressing. Nevertheless, a modern student might have little reason to pay close attention to Green's theory of knowledge were it not for the necessary connection he held to exist between his epistemology and his ethics and his failure to state fully his theory of knowledge within the body of his ethical thought. Whatever the actual reason for this failure – and it may have simply been the brevity of his life – writers who have not examined his epistemology have not fully appreciated the rest of his system, while those who have studied it have either been solely concerned with this area of his philosophy or have not adequately emphasized those points which are necessary to an understanding of his social and political thought.[2] This chapter therefore pre-

1 Ann R. Cacoullos, *Thomas Hill Green: Philosopher of Rights* (New York: Twayne Publishers, 1974), p. 34
2 The failure to interpret satisfactorily Green's metaphysical thought may be due in part to the complexity and awkwardness of his style. In replying to Green's attack on him, Herbert Spencer, noting the lapse of time between the appearance of Green's articles and his reply, remarked that

sents a detailed examination of the philosophical foundations of Green's work – both his theory of knowledge and the roots of his ethical system as understood in light of this theory. However, because it is not my primary concern to analyse critically the theoretical basis of his thought, this chapter will be in the main expository.

I

Metaphysics, for Green, 'is simply the consideration of what is implied in the fact of our knowing or coming to know a world, or, conversely, in the fact of there being a world for us to know.'[3] The starting-point for such an enquiry, in his view, is the question 'whether a being that was merely a result of natural forces could form a theory of those forces as explaining himself.'[4] For Green, the answer is a resounding No, whether the attempt to explain human knowledge as a natural phenomenon is based on an examination of the individual or of the evolutionary development of mankind as a whole.[5] Moreover, only a negative answer to this question can form the basis of a theory of ethics:

Can the knowledge of nature be itself a part or product of nature, in that sense of nature in which it is said to be an object of knowledge? This is our first question. If it is answered in the negative, we shall at least have satisfied ourselves that man, in respect of the function called knowledge, is not merely a child of nature. We shall have ascertained the presence in him of a spiritual principle not natural, and a specific function of this principle in rendering knowledge possible. The way will then be so far cleared for the further question which leads us, in the language of Kant, from the Critique of Speculative to that of Practical Reason: the question whether the same principle has not another expression than that which appears in the determination of experience and through it in our knowledge of a world – an expression

he had been busy with other work, but that his 'wish to avoid hindrance [was] supported partly by the thought that very few would read a discussion so difficult to follow.' Herbert Spencer, 'Professor Green's Explanations,' *Contemporary Review*, XXXIX (February 1881), p. 305. See also, John Addington Symonds, *The Letters of John Addington Symonds*, 3 vols, ed. Herbert M. Schueller and Robert L. Peters (Detroit: Wayne State University Press, 1968-9), II, p. 333.

A further difficulty arises from the fact that much of Green's work is in the form of lecture notes which he was personally unable to edit for publication.

3 *Spencer & Lewes*, sec. 2
4 PE, sec. 8
5 'Spencer, in a word, only tells us, taking a longer, more roundabout road than the earlier empiricists followed, using the life of the race instead of that of an individual, that experience is the source of knowledge, while he has a theory of experience which would not allow it to be the source of anything.' John Dewey, 'The Philosophy of Thomas Hill Green,' *Andover Review*, XI: No. 64 (April 1889), p. 343. See *Spencer & Lewes*, secs. 68, 89, 90, 93, 96; and PE, sec. 114.

which consists in the consciousness of a moral ideal and the determination of human action thereby.[6]

The basic error of the argument that human knowledge is a result of natural processes, according to Green, arises from the supposition of an antithesis between the real and the work of the mind and consists in endowing the 'real' – feeling or sensation – with a reality it can have only through the work of the mind, or thought.[7] This error is an understandable one:

In first reflecting on our knowledge of a world, we always regard the facts known as existing quite independently of the activity by means of which they are known. Since it is obvious that the facts of the world do not come into existence when this or that person becomes acquainted with them, so long as we conceive of no intellectual action but that which this or that person exercises, we necessarily regard the existence or occurrence of the facts as independent of intellectual action. Hence arises the antithesis between the known or knowable world and the subject capable of knowing it, as between two existences independent of each other, or of which the former is at any rate independent of the latter. The mind is supposed to derive its materials from, and to act only in response to, the action of the world upon it; but the relations which it establishes between the materials, so derived, in its processes of distinction and comparison, of conception, judgment, and discourse, are supposed to be quite different, and to have a different source, from the relations between things or matters of fact in the world known.[8]

In truth, Green holds, feeling and thought are both necessary to constitute reality; neither by itself is sufficient to form a fact:

We admit that mere thought can no more produce the facts of feeling, than mere feeling can generate thought. But we deny that there is really such a thing as 'mere feeling' or 'mere thought.' We hold that these phrases represent abstractions to which no reality corresponds, either in the facts of the world or in the consciousness to which these facts are relative. We can attach no meaning to 'reality' as applied to the world of phenomena, but that of existence under definite and unalterable relations; and we find that it is only for a thinking consciousness that such relations can subsist. Reality of feeling, abstracted from thought, is abstracted from the condition of its being a reality.[9]

6 PE, sec. 8. Cf. secs 2, 52; and *Lectures on Kant*, sec. 72.
7 See, for example, *Hume I*, secs 85, 113, 153; *Spencer & Lewes*, sec. 95; and, 'Review of J. Caird,' *Works*, III, p. 145.
8 PE, sec. 34
9 PE, sec. 51. Cf. secs 34, 48, 50; *Hume I*, sec. 173; *Lectures on Kant*, secs 4, 114; and, *Spencer & Lewes*, secs 29, 33, 51

Whether we consciously realize it or not, we can only know an object – it only has an identity for us – through its relations to ourselves and other objects. The pen with which I write, for example, is what it is for me by virtue of its similarity to and difference from other objects around it. On the most rudimentary level, it is only an object of my knowledge because I, the knowing subject, distinguish it from myself.[10] In addition, the paper on which I write, the desk on which the paper rests, the pencil I sometimes use instead of the pen – all of these objects, and a myriad of others – contribute to that which I know as a pen. However, the mere sensation of light which reaches my eyes from the pen does not bear these relations. Thought without sensation can convey no reality, but thought is necessary to give meaning and form to the sensation by relating it to other sensations I have had in the past. Indeed, I, as a thinking subject, never really see the pen *except* as the pen, and hence as determined by relations.[11] Even the most insignificant feeling I have is qualified by relations.[12]

Every individual object of knowledge, therefore, may be viewed as a focus of relations – 'a congeries of related facts'[13] – and, as such, it is also a universal:

Relation is to us such a familiar fact that we are apt to forget that it involves all the mystery, if it be a mystery, of the existence of many in one. Whether we say that a related thing is one in itself, manifold in respect of its relations, or that there is one relation between bodies – and one expression or the other we must employ in stating the simplest facts – we are equally

---

10 'The Philosophy of Aristotle,' *Works*, III, pp. 63-4; *Hume I*, sec. 144
11 *Hume I*, sec. 297; *Lectures on Logic*, secs 16, 17, 52, 87, 140; *Spencer & Lewes*, secs 35, 134
12 *Hume I*, secs 24, 330; *Spencer & Lewes*, sec. 36; PE, sec. 64
   A number of writers have been critical of Green's theory of relations for various reasons. Balfour, for example, argues that relations are so all-pervasive in Green's system that they leave nothing to relate. Arthur James Balfour, *The Foundations of Belief* (New York: Longmans, Green, 1895), p. 145; and his 'Green's Metaphysics of Knowledge,' *Mind*, IX: No. 33 (Jan. 1884), pp. 76-8. G. Watts Cunningham holds that Green vacillates between two positions, in some places arguing that relations are supplied by the relating consciousness, in others that they come with the related sensations. *The Idealist Argument in Recent British and American Philosophy* (New York and London: The Century Co., 1933), pp. 354-7. J.H. Randall maintains that, despite his attempt to remove the opposition between thought and feeling, Green himself reproduces it since he must ultimately hold that there is a world and a relating consciousness, matter and mind, as two distinct entities. 'T.H. Green: The Development of English Thought from J.S. Mill to F.H. Bradley,' *Journal of the History of Ideas*, XXVII: No. 2 (April-June 1966), pp. 222-4.
   None of these criticisms is especially damaging to Green's system. The first two are simply misreadings. Randall on the other hand seems to miss the point that, although there may be two separate entities, there can only be a reality *for us* through their interaction. Thus, really, in the only sense in which there can be a 'really' for us, there is no antithesis. Nevertheless, there is validity in the view that Green's theory is not totally devoid of dualisms, as we shall see.
13 PE, sec. 64. Cf. *Spencer & Lewes*, sec. 108.

affirming the unity of the manifold. Abstract the many relations from the one thing, and there is nothing. They, being many, determine or constitute its definite unity. It is not the case that it first exists in its unity, and then is brought into various relations. Without the relations it would not exist at all. In like manner the one relation is a unity of the many things. They, in their manifold being, make the one relation.[14]

Accordingly, in contrast to the empiricists, Green believed that thought is a process from the abstract to the concrete, from the less to the more determinate. As our knowledge of an object grows, we in effect perceive it in an ever greater number and variety of relations.[15] Moreover, knowledge is not merely the passive receiving of external impressions portrayed by the adherents of the empirical tradition but an active, constitutive, creative process.[16]

For Green, then, as for Kant, 'the understanding makes nature'[17]; without the relating activity of the mind there would be no knowledge for us. However, as merely relating, mind would not be adequate to its task. Sensations are, by definition, fleeting; whatever form they take (as sight, sound, etc.), they pass almost as soon as they are felt. Therefore, their relation or mutual determination implies their presence to an abiding or permanent unit that distinguishes itself from them, a mind or consciousness that persists throughout their succession in time and space and is thus able to consider them simultaneously[18]:

The members of a relation must exist together. But of the feelings between which we assert a relation one is past or passing before the other begins, and this other has no sooner begun than it is over. I strike one note of music and then another and assert a relation of difference between them, but only because for the comparing subject they are present together – only because for it they are *not* what as feelings in time they *are*, viz. successive.[19]

14 PE, sec. 28. Cf. 'The Philosophy of Aristotle,' *Works*, III, pp. 69-70; *Hume I*, sec. 329; and *Lectures on Logic*, sec. 28

15 'The Philosophy of Aristotle,' *Works*, III, pp. 52, 53, 59-60, 65; *Hume I*, secs 40, 95; *Lectures on Logic*, sec. 32

16 'The Force of Circumstances,' *Works*, III, pp. 4-5; 'An Estimate of the Value and Influence of Works of Fiction in Modern Times,' *Works*, III, p. 22; 'Popular Philosophy in its Relation to Life,' *Works*, III, pp. 95-6, 112; *Hume I*, secs 8, 34, 113; *Hume II*, sec. 64; *Spencer & Lewes*, sec. 6; PE, sec. 64. Cf. Oskar Günther, *Das Verhältnis der Ethik Thomas Hill Greens zu derjenigen Kants* (PHD dissertation, Dresden: Theodor Beyer, 1915), p. 46; and J.H. Muirhead, *The Service of the State* (London: John Murray, 1908), pp. 9-10.

17 PE, secs 11, 19

18 'The Philosophy of Aristotle,' *Works*, III, pp. 52, 63; *Hume I*, secs 212, 249, 314, 318; *Lectures on Logic*, secs 10, 11, 18, 27, 124; *Lectures on Kant*, secs 10, 11; *Spencer & Lewes*, secs 77, 88, 101; PE, secs 29, 31, 64; 'Review of J. Caird,' *Works*, III, p. 145

19 *Lectures on Logic*, sec. 61

We may say further of this permanent self or subject that it cannot be a feeling or any other natural event because these, as transitory, cannot be permanent. Similarly, the self cannot be a succession of feelings or events, because a succession is itself a relation of passing sensations implying the presence to them of a permanent self. Nor can it be the product of a series of feelings or events, since as a product it must follow them and hence cannot be present to them. In short, the self is neither the result of natural forces nor determined by them, but as prerequisite to a knowledge of these forces it must be present to them.[20]

To this point Green's discussion is a demonstration of the inaccuracy of the antithesis between the real and the work of the mind. However, having removed the basis of this antithesis, he has at the same time removed the basis of the generally accepted distinction between fact and illusion, i.e. that the unreal is opposed to the real as being merely the product of thought. What we actually do, Green contends, in testing the reality of an object, is not to oppose it to the work of the mind, for all reality is the product of thought, but to test its consistency with the unalterable order of nature.

According to Green, 'feelings which are conceived as facts are already conceived as constituents of nature. The same presence of the thinking subject to, and distinction of itself from, the feelings, which renders them knowable *facts*, renders them members of a world which is one throughout its changes.'[21] That is to say, since the reality of an object or event is constituted by its relations to other objects or events, it is but a logical deduction from this to maintain that, in establishing that a particular object is *real*, we also establish that it is connected to and determined by a whole series of other objects, which must therefore together form a system or order of facts. On this account, the reality of a new 'fact' is determined on the basis of its compatibility or incompatibility with the facts that have already been established, with the whole system of those facts. Moreover, this system must be unalterable; otherwise we could not be certain that what is a fact today was so yesterday and will remain so tomorrow.[22] To be sure, there may be change in such a system, but it must be uniform change according to unchangeable laws.[23]

Rather than creating an obstacle to the distinction of fact from fancy, Green holds that his theory is necessary to this distinction:

On the recognition of relations as constituting the nature of ideas rests the possibility of any tenable theory of their reality. An isolated idea could be neither real nor unreal. Apart from a

---

20 *Spencer & Lewes*, secs 31, 57, 59, 62, 66; PE, secs 16, 18
21 *Hume I*, sec. 321
22 *Hume I*, sec. 111; *Lectures on Logic*, sec. 112; PE, secs 24, 33
23 *Lectures on Logic*, secs 11, 28

definite order of relation we may suppose (if we like) that it would *be*, but it would certainly not be real; and as little could it be unreal, since unreality can only result from the confusion in our consciousness of one order of relation with another.[24]

Indeed, the very possibility of our quest for knowledge is predicated on the assumption of such an unalterable world of experience.[25]

However, such an unchanging order of nature, as knowable, requires a consciousness, permanent throughout the succession of natural events. Just as our knowledge, a knowledge of related objects and events, implies the presence to them of an abiding mind or consciousness, permanent throughout their succession, the related objects and events of nature similarly imply such a mind. That this knowing subject cannot be a particular human consciousness follows from the fact of human mortality. A particular human mind cannot have been present to that which preceded its birth, but such events are as much a part of the system of nature known to this mind as are those events which it itself experiences; they equally determine and are determined by the other members of the system.[26] Moreover, Green argues, if each of us 'made' nature for ourselves, 'the "objectivity" of nature would doubtless disappear; there would be as many "natures" as men.'[27]

It is quite true that the relations which form the object-matter of our knowledge do not come into being with the experience which I or any one may happen to have of them, but on the other hand, except as relations of what is relative to consciousness, they are simply nothing; nor, unless we suppose consciousness with its world to come into existence over and over again as this man or that becomes conscious, is there any difficulty in reconciling these two propositions.[28]

The reconciliation of these two propositions, for Green, is to be found in the eternal consciousness – the spiritual principle in nature – the single, self-conscious

24 *Hume I*, sec. 188
25 *Hume I*, sec. 149; *Lectures on Logic*, sec. 127; *Lectures on Kant*, sec. 4; PE, sec. 26
26 'There is no meaning in speaking of a series of events, "revealed to us by science" as antecedent conditions of life and sentience, which must have taken place when as yet life and sentience were not, as if they did not belong to our phenomenal world, "the cosmos of our experience". They are conditions of what we experience, determined just as much by relation to what we experience as it by relation to them. Limit "our experience" to the succession of our feelings, and there is no "world of experience". Extend it so as to mean that which determines our feeling, and it must include conditions antecedent to the appearance of sentient life just as much as any other. If "science" reveals such conditions, the right inference to draw is, not that the world is independent of thought, but that thought, the condition of there being such conditions, does not come into being as a development of life and sentience.' *Lectures on Kant*, sec. 63
27 Ibid., sec. 26
28 *Spencer & Lewes*, sec. 108

subject, whose presence to the totality and multiplicity of nature constitutes its reality as a system.[29] And *our* knowledge of this system suggests to Green that 'our conception of an order of nature, and the relations which form that order, have a common spiritual source'[30]; that the world of experience, 'as it exists only in relation to an eternal and self-conscious mind, so is knowable by us only because this mind constitutes the "me" in each of us.'[31] 'Our reason' Green contends '*is* this eternal thinking subject,'[32] in 'a limited mode.'[33] 'The eternal subject is me as ego, but as an ego determining all phenomena. If it were not me, my knowledge would be impossible; there would be no nature for me. If it were me in its full reality, as the subject determining all phenomena, my knowledge would be all knowledge.'[34] The growth of human knowledge, therefore, is the process in which 'the consciousness for which the cosmos eternally exists becomes partially ours.'[35] Man gradually becomes the 'vehicle'[36] in which the 'reproduction'[37] of the eternal mind takes place.[38]

The exact nature of the eternal consciousness cannot be determined. We know that it is self-distinguishing, as is the human consciousness, for only as self-distinguishing is it able to stand apart, so to speak, from the cosmos of experience, both in time and space, in order to link its members in an all-embracing system. Furthermore, as standing apart from this system, it is not itself determined by it:

We are further entitled to say of it, negatively, that the relations by which, through its action, phenomena are determined are not relations *of* it – not relations by which it is itself determined. They arise out of its presence to phenomena, or the presence of phenomena to it, but the very condition of their thus arising is that the unifying consciousness which constitutes them should not itself be one of the objects so related. The relation of events to each other as

29 *Lectures on Logic*, secs 124, 127; *Lectures on Kant*, sec. 73; *Spencer & Lewes*, secs 87, 119; 'Review of J. Caird,' *Works*, III, p. 145; PE, secs 32, 52, 69
30 PE, sec. 33
31 *Lectures on Logic*, sec. 21
32 *Lectures on Kant*, sec. 64
33 PE, sec. 51. 'The conclusion to which we are brought by the foregoing argument is that man, as knowing a cosmos or rational world, is mind knowing and discovering mind.' Percival Chubb, 'The Significance of Thomas Hill Green's Philosophical and Religious Teaching,' *Journal of Speculative Philosophy*, XXII: Nos 1-2 (Jan.-April 1888), p. 12
34 *Lectures on Kant*, sec. 26
35 *Spencer & Lewes*, sec. 104
36 'The Philosophy of Aristotle,' *Works*, III, p. 73. *Lectures on Logic*, sec. 21; PE, sec. 67. Cf. 'The Force of Circumstances,' *Works*, III, p. 5: 'the living receptacle.'
37 PE, secs 71, 73, 74. This process is also referred to as 'actualization' (*Hume I*, sec. 152), 'self-realization' (PE, secs 74, 82), and 'revelation' (*Lectures on Kant*, sec. 6).
38 'In other language, one Mind expresses itself *in* Man and, through Nature, *to* Man; and our mental growth is, in fact, our progressive assimilation of the Cosmic Mind, or the Cosmic Mind becoming more and more articulate in us.' Chubb, 'The Significance of Thomas Hill Green's ... Teaching,' p. 12

in time implies their equal presence to a subject which is not in time. There could be no such thing as time if there were not a self-consciousness which is not in time. As little could there be a relation of objects as outside each other, or in space, if they were not equally related to a subject which they are not outside; a subject of which outsideness to anything is not a possible attribute; which by its synthetic action constitutes that relation but is not itself determined by it.[39]

At this point we may return to Green's question posed at the outset of this inquiry: 'Can the knowledge of nature be itself a part or product of nature, in that sense of nature in which it is said to be an object of knowledge?'[40] Clearly, for Green, the eternal consciousness is not a part of nature, nor can we account for it as we do natural objects and events. 'By calling the principle not natural we mean that it is neither included among the phenomena which through its presence to them form a nature, nor consists in their series, nor is itself determined by any of the relations which it constitutes among them.'[41] In other words, because it makes knowledge possible, it can be neither a member of the order of nature nor a product of it.

To be sure, the eternal subject may be described as the 'cause' of nature. However, cause in this sense is not to be confused with a cause within the order of experience, which, itself caused or conditioned by other antecedent events, is merely a member of the natural system.[42] Rather, the eternal consciousness as cause is an unconditioned 'free cause,' and man, as 'partaker'[43] of this consciousness, is himself a 'free cause.' 'Thus, while still confining our view to man's achievement in knowledge, we are entitled to say that in himself, i.e., in respect of that principle through which he at once is a self and distinguishes himself as such, he exerts a *free activity* – an activity which is not in time, not a link in the chain of natural becoming, which has no antecedents other than itself but is self-originated.'[44] It should be noted that man *is* determined by the world in which he lives in the sense that he would not be what he is – he would not have the identity he has – were it not for his relations both to other individuals and to natural circumstances. But the relations by which he is thus qualified are relations established through the action of his own intelligence: he is *self*-determined.[45]

If, then, human knowledge is an expression of the eternal subject – and Green has demonstrated, to his own satisfaction at least, that this is so – human knowledge

39 PE, sec. 52
40 PE, sec. 8
41 PE, sec. 57
42 PE, sec. 76
43 'An Estimate of the Value and Influence of Works of Fiction in Modern Times,' *Works*, III, p. 22
44 PE, sec. 82
45 PE, secs 74, 76, 77

itself cannot be explained as a result or development of natural events; it cannot have a natural history.[46] Indeed, the very existence of a science of nature is itself proof of the existence of a non-natural principle in man and nature which makes that science possible.[47]

Finally, because the human subject shares a common mind or self with the eternal subject, it is conscious of there being a perfect knowledge of the universe, it 'can enjoy the consciousness of its perfect original.'[48] However, because it is housed within an animal organism, its knowledge must be limited: 'It is not our sentience that is the condition of there being for us a phenomenal world, though the fact that we are sentient (and, so far, merely parts of this world) limits (renders inadequate) the mode in which we understand it.'[49]

Neither the thing as we at any time conceive it, nor the thing as we feel it, is the thing in the *fulness* of its reality. I have a conception of a flower, and upon the occurrence of a sensation, which I interpret by means of this conception, I judge 'there is a real flower'; but the flower is *really* much more than the relations which I had previously conceived *plus* the present relation to sense. But this 'more' still lies in relations which can only exist for a conceiving mind, and which my mind is in process of appropriating. The great mistake lies in regarding a conception as a fixed quantity, a 'bundle of attributes'. In truth a

46 *Hume I*, sec. 200; cf. PE, secs 50, 51, 54.
47 Green's 'eternal consciousness' has been a source of wide dispute among commentators. The most serious objection is that raised by Andrew Seth in his *Hegelianism and Personality* (Edinburgh and London: William Blackwood, 1887). He argues that the eternal self is merely a 'unifying principle' which has 'no nature of its own apart from what it does in relation to the manifold world.' This makes it 'no more than a *focus imaginarius* into which the multiplex relations which constitute the intelligible world return. Such a focus or principle of unity enables us to round off our theory with an appearance of personality, but it does not satisfy in any real sense the requirements of Theism' (p. 26). Accordingly, what Green does 'is neither more nor less than to hypostatize an abstraction ... There no doubt may be an eternally complete self-consciousness which holds a creative relation to our own, and much of Green's theory of the universe may be substantially true; but if so its truth must be established upon other lines' (p. 30, esp. pp. 23-30).

For further discussion of this criticism, see John Dewey, 'On Some Current Conceptions of the Term "Self,"' *Mind*, XV: No. 57 (Jan. 1890), pp. 73-4; R.B.C. Johnson, *The Metaphysics of Knowledge* (PHD dissertation), *Princeton Contributions to Philosophy*, I: No. 3 (April 1900), pp. 37-48; J. Charles McKirachan, *The Temporal and the Eternal in the Philosophy of Thomas Hill Green* (PHD dissertation, Princeton, 1941), pp. 79-84; J.H. Muirhead, *The Platonic Tradition in Anglo-Saxon Philosophy* (London: George Allen and Unwin, 1931), pp. 204-5. Cf. J.H. Randall, 'T.H. Green,' p. 222; and Howard Selsam, *T.H. Green: Critic of Empiricism* (PHD dissertation, New York, 1930), pp. 96-7.
48 'The Influence of Civilization on Genius,' *Works*, III, p. 11. Cf. 'Christian Dogma,' *Works*, III, pp. 182-3.
49 *Lectures on Kant*, sec. 63

conception, as the thought of an object *under relations*, is from its very nature in constant expansion.[50]

As a sentient being, man occupies a certain position in time and space, which he can never fully escape. Accordingly, he can never be permanently present to the totality of relations that determines a particular object or event, not to mention the system of nature as a whole.[51] Nevertheless, the progress of our knowledge represents the 'struggle' of consciousness 'to work itself free' from its limitations.[52]

2

One of the least understood areas of Green's system is the relationship between his epistemology and his moral philosophy. The key to an appreciation of this relationship lies in the consideration that, for Green, desires are comparable to sensations, that just as natural sensations or feelings form the basis of our knowledge so desires are central to human or moral action. Thus, he argues, 'the animal system is not organic merely to feeling of the kind just spoken of as receptive, to *impressions* ... It is organic also to *wants*, and to impulses for the satisfaction of those wants, which may be in many cases occasioned by impressions of the kind mentioned, but which constitute quite a different function of the animal system.'[53] In the same way, therefore, as *mere* feeling combines with thought to mould a world of experience for man, *mere* appetite – or want, or desire (Green uses the terms interchangeably) – undergoes a transformation by virtue of its presence to human consciousness and produces a world of moral activity.

50 *Lectures on Logic*, sec. 29, Cf. sec. 11; 'The Philosophy of Aristotle,' *Works*, III, pp. 72-3; *Spencer & Lewes*, sec. 119.
51 PE, sec. 72; 'An Estimate of the Value and Influence of Works of Fiction in Modern Times,' *Works*, III, p. 22; 'Review of J. Caird,' *Works*, III, p. 145
52 'Christian Dogma,' *Works*, III, p. 182. Cf. 'The Influence of Civilization on Genius,' *Works*, III, p. 11. 'To the individual man, no doubt, the absoluteness of his limitations never wholly vanishes. The dream that it can do so is the frenzy of philosophy.' 'The Philosophy of Aristotle,' *Works*, III, p. 86.
   Green leaves us with a sense of the fundamental inscrutability of this process: 'The question why there should be this reproduction, is indeed as unanswerable as every form of the question why the world as a whole should be what it is. Why any detail of the world is what it is, we can explain by reference to other details which determine it; but why the whole should be what it is, why the mind which the world implies should exhibit itself in a world at all, why it should make certain processes of that world organic to a reproduction of itself under limitations which the use of such organs involves – these are questions which, owing perhaps to those very limitations, we are equally unable to avoid asking and to answer. We have to content ourselves with saying that, strange as it may seem, it is so. Taking all the facts of the case together, we cannot express them otherwise.' PE, sec. 82
53 PE, sec. 85

According to Green, just as to know a natural object or event is really to know it in terms of its relations to other objects or events in the system of nature, so to experience a desire is really to experience it in terms of its relations to the individual's perceived personal good. In other words, the desire is transformed from an isolated feeling to a member of a related whole, and its character is fundamentally altered. If I experience hunger, for example, that hunger is not *mere* hunger, Green holds, but hunger related to and determined by me, because I can think about the hunger, distinguish myself and my other desires from it, and realize that it is *I* who am hungry. That is to say, in satisfying myself, I take into consideration a whole range of elements other than the hunger. Thus, if I am ill, I will likely not eat certain foods; if I am in a hurry or occupied with an important matter, I might refrain from eating altogether; and so on. The appetite, in short – whether 'of a purely animal origin' or 'of distinctively human origin'[54] – does not exist in a vacuum but is related to other factors, and in fact, Green contends, it cannot be experienced otherwise. In Green's terminology, 'mere want' becomes 'the consciousness of a wanted object.'[55]

However, this is only true because the desire occurs to a self-determining subject which is present throughout the succession of desires, and which can therefore remove the desire from and relate it to the other members of the succession.[56] 'It is thus equally important to bear in mind' Green writes 'that there is a real unity in all a man's desires, a common ground of them all, and that this real unity or common ground is simply the man's self, as conscious of itself and consciously seeking in the satisfaction of desires the satisfaction of itself.'[57] In addition, Green points out, the desiring self of man is the same as his knowing self and is, similarly, a reproduction of the eternal consciousness. 'The self-conscious principle, implied in the presentation of self-satisfaction as an object ... is identical with the principle in virtue of which there is for us a nature.'[58]

Unlike the object of knowledge, the object of desire does not already exist:

54 PE, sec. 86. On 'distinctively human' desires, cf. PE, sec. 126: 'Our envies, jealousies, and ambitions – whatever the resemblance between their outward signs and certain expressions of emotion in animals – are all in their proper nature distinctively human, because all founded on interests possible only to self-conscious beings. We cannot separate such passions from their exciting causes. Take away those occasions of them which arise out of intercourse as persons with persons, and the passions themselves as we know them disappear. The advantages which I envy in my neighbour, the favour of society or of a particular person which I lose and he wins and which makes me jealous of him, the superiority in form or power or place of which the imagination excites my ambition – these would have no more existence for an agent not self-conscious, or not dealing with other self-conscious agents, than colour has for the blind.'

55 See, for example, *Lectures on Kant*, secs 78, 79, 81; PE, secs 85, 86.

56 'Popular Philosophy in its Relation to Life,' *Works*, III, pp. 104-5; *Hume II*, sec. 8; *Lectures on Kant*, sec. 81; PE, secs 85, 86, 98, 120, 125

57 PE, sec. 129

58 *Lectures on Kant*, sec. 79. The similarity between the faculties of knowledge and desire is also expressed by Green as follows: 'The element common to both lies in the consciousness of self

The sensible object is something which is; the wanted object (the filling of the want) is something which *is to be* (has yet to be brought into existence). In this lies the distinction between 'sein' and 'sollen' in the most elementary form. As intelligent experience, and with it nature and knowledge, result from the presentation of sensible objects and their connection in one universe (a connection which results from that same relation to a self-conscious subject which is the condition of their presentation as objects), so practice results from the presentation of wanted objects, objects to be brought into existence. But whereas in knowledge the sensible object carries its reality with it (in being presented at all it is presented as real), in practice the wanted object is one to which reality has yet to be given ... Thus the world of practice depends on man in quite a different sense from that in which nature does. We commonly speak of nature as wholly independent of man. This is not true in the sense that there could be nature (the nature that we know) without intelligent consciousness; but it is true in the sense that, given the consciousness of sensible objects, it does not depend on any exercise of our powers whether they shall become real or no; they are already real. On the other hand, in the world of practice, consciousness of an object is prior to its reality, and it depends on a certain exercise of our powers, determined by that consciousness, whether the object shall become real or no.[59]

The wanted object, be it noted, is the filling of the want. If I desire a particular thing, it makes no difference, according to Green, whether it already physically exists. It does not yet exist *as mine*, and hence it has yet to be determined through its relation to me – it has yet to become a part of my moral universe.

The consciousness of a wanted object, therefore, is at the same time a motive – 'an idea of an end, which a self-conscious subject presents to itself, and which it strives and tends to realize'[60] – which moves man to action in an effort to actualize his object. Furthermore, this object is at all times a personal end, the idea, that is, of a better state of the self to be achieved, and one in which the subject is the driving, determining force:

The want, no doubt, may remain along with the new result – the motive, properly so called – which arises from its relation to self-consciousness, but it is not a part of it. Hunger, for instance, may survive along with the motive, involving some form of self-reference, which arises out of it in the self-conscious man – whether that motive be the desire to relieve himself from pain, or to give himself pleasure, or to qualify himself for work, or to provide himself the means of living – but hunger neither is that motive nor a part of it. If it were the resulting act would not be moral but instinctive. There would be no moral agency in it. It

and a world as in a sense opposed to each other, and in the conscious effort to overcome this
opposition.' PE, sec. 130. Cf. secs 132, 133; and 'The Philosophy of Aristotle,' *Works*, III, p. 86.
59 *Lectures on Kant*, sec. 78; cf. PE, secs 86, 87.
60 PE, sec. 87

would not be the man that did it, but the hunger or some 'force of nature' in him. The motive in every imputable act for which the agent is conscious on reflection that he is answerable, is a desire for personal good in some form or other; and, however much the idea of what the personal good for the time is may be affected by the pressure of animal want, this want is no more a part or component of the desire than is the sensation of light or colour, which I receive in looking at this written line, a component part of my perception in reading it.[61]

Motive, in turn, gives rise to an act of will that consists in the identification of the self with a particular object of desire (among competing objects) as representing, for the time, the individual's greatest good and his subsequent endeavour to attain self-sastisfaction through the realization of this object.[62] The direction in which the will is usually determined – the type of objects in which self-satisfaction is for the most part sought – constitutes the individual's character:

Just as there is a growth of knowledge in man, though knowledge is only possible through the action in him of the eternal subject, so is there a growth of character, though the possibility of there being a character in the moral sense is similarly conditioned. It grows with the ever-new adoption of desired objects by a self-presenting and, in that sense, eternal subject as its personal good. The act of adoption is the act of a subject which has not come to be; the act itself is not in time in the sense of being an event determined by previous events; but its product is a further step in that order of becoming which we call the formation of a character, in the growth of some habit of will.[63]

We have already seen that, for Green, man as knower of the cosmos of experience is free in so far as, because of the reproduction in him of the eternal consciousness, he is not himself determined by nature. On the contrary, it is through the action of his understanding that the various parts of the natural world are related to form a system. Similarly, in all willing, in the effort to achieve self-satisfaction – no matter what the particular object is – man is free in the sense that he is self-determined.[64] Unlike the merely sentient animals who, as members of nature themselves, are related to and hence determined by their appetites – which as sensations are also

61 PE, sec. 91. Cf. secs 88, 89, 95, 96; and *Lectures on Kant*, sec. 79.
62 *Lectures on Kant*, sec. 122; PPO, sec. 6; PE, secs 102, 146, 147, 153, 175
63 PE, sec. 101. Cf. 'The Philosophy of Aristotle,' *Works*, III, p. 86; *Lectures on Kant*, sec. 122
64 'Since in all willing a man is his own subject, the will is always free. Or, more properly, a man in willing is necessarily free since willing constitutes freedom and "free will" is the pleonasm "free freedom."' 'On the Different Senses of "Freedom" as Applied to Will and to the Moral Progress of Man,' *Works*, II, sec. 1. Nettleship comments: 'Freedom, then, is one constituent element of personality; it *is* personality in one of its aspects.' R.L. Nettleship, 'Professor T.H. Green: In Memoriam,' *Contemporary Review*, XLI (May 1882), p. 876

members of the system of nature – man is not so related.[65] Rather, as discussed above, his desires become what they are through their presence to him as a self-conscious subject. Through his motives he determines them as his objects, potential elements in his perceived personal good – indeed, he cannot otherwise experience them as desires – whereas the only relations by which he is determined are those he consciously makes for himself. 'So far from free action being unmotived, it is rather determination by motives, properly understood, that constitutes freedom.'[66]

Green draws a sharp line between instinctive and self-directed or moral actions. In the former category he includes 'actions done in sleep (resulting from animal tendencies), or strictly under compulsion, or from accident.'[67] They all have this in common, that they are performed unconsciously, so to speak, with no determination of the object by the subject; the agent is blindly governed by external forces. 'If in our waking and sane life we are capable of such a merely animal experience at all, it at any rate does not affect us for the better or worse as men. It has no bearing on the state of soul or character to which the terms good or bad in the moral sense are applied.'[68] On the contrary, activity consciously directed to objects forming the agent's perceived personal good, of which only a self-determining subject is capable, is what constitutes his moral nature. In such activity man is free to direct himself to objects which are virtuous or vicious and, for this reason, he sees himself as author of his actions and as responsible for them.[69] 'We should be as incapable of error as of true knowledge, of sin as of moral perfection, if we could not place ourselves outside our sensations and distinguish ourselves from our desires.'[70] In such activity, therefore, man expresses his moral freedom.

In this context Green argues that the faculties of man should not be viewed as separate and competing. Thus, in his view, it is meaningless to speak of doing something against one's will. Rather, 'there is one subject or spirit, which desires in

65 *Hume II*, sec. 4; *Lectures on Kant*, secs 82, 92; PE, sec. 100. It is important to bear in mind that Green employed the terms 'related' ('relation') and 'determined' ('determination') interchangeably.

66 *Lectures on Kant*, sec. 83. Cf. sec. 113; PE, sec. 102; 'On the Different Senses of "Freedom,"' *Works*, II, sec. 13.
    Green sometimes speaks as if man *were* determined by external forces. For example: 'Without the constitutive action of man or his will the objects do not exist; apart from determination by some object neither he nor his will would be more than an unreal abstraction.' *Lectures on Kant*, addition to sec. 124. However, in being so determined, man is, according to Green, determined by relations of his own making, relations into which he places himself, and thus remains self-determined.

67 *Lectures on Kant*, sec. 113. Cf. 'The Word is Nigh Thee,' *Works*, III, p. 224; and PE, secs 92, 93.

68 PE, sec. 125

69 PE, sec. 96; *Lectures on Kant*, sec. 113

70 'The Philosophy of Aristotle,' *Works*, III, pp. 86-7

all a man's experiences of desire, understands in all operations of his intelligence, wills in all acts of his willing.'[71] 'The will is simply the man. Any act of will is the expression of the man as he at the time is.'[72]

Similarly, Green contends, neither a man's character nor his circumstances can adversely affect his moral freedom. Character, as described above, is the man as represented in his acts of will; 'moral action is the expression of a man's character.'[73]

It is strictly a contradiction, then, to say that an action which a man's character determines, or which expresses his character, is one that he cannot help doing. It represents him as standing in a relation to external agency, while doing the act, in which he does not stand if his character determines it. We may say, if we like, without any greater error than that of inappropriate phraseology, that, given the agent's character and circumstances as they at any time are, the action 'cannot help being done,' if by that we merely mean that the action is as necessarily related to the character and circumstances as any event to the sum of its conditions. The meaning in that case is not untrue; but the expression is inappropriate, for it implies a kind of personification of the action. It speaks of the action as abstracted from the agent, in terms only appropriate to an agent whose powers are directed by a force not his own.[74]

The history of the individual's past desires and actions may, to a greater or lesser extent, determine his present choices. Still, throughout this past activity, he has been a self-conscious subject, and therefore self-determining. His present actions, then, are themselves determined solely by the subject himself.[75] As for circumstances, Green holds that these have no significant effect on moral freedom:

It is not necessary to moral freedom that, on the part of the person to whom it belongs, there should be an indeterminate possibility of becoming and doing anything and everything. A man's possibilities of doing and becoming at any moment of his life are as thoroughly conditioned as those of an animal or a plant; but the conditions are different. The conditions that determine what a plant or animal or any natural agent shall do or become, are not objects that it presents to itself; not objects in which it seeks self-satisfaction. On the other hand, whatever conditions the man's possibilities does so through his self-consciousness. The climate in which he lives, the food and drink accessible to him, and other strictly physical circum-

71 PE, sec. 117
72 PE, sec. 153. Cf. Book II, Chapter II, esp. secs 117, 120, 130, 133-6, 146-7; and 'On the Different Senses of "Freedom,"' *Works*, II, sec. 13.
73 PE, sec. 107
74 PE, sec. 109; cf. sec. 108.
75 *Lectures on Kant*, sec. 87; 'On the Different Senses of "Freedom,"' *Works*, II, sec. 14; PE, secs 99, 102

stances, no doubt make a difference to him; but it is only through the medium of a conception of personal good, only so far as the man out of his relations to them makes to himself certain objects in which he seeks self-satisfaction, that they make a difference to him as a man or moral being. It is only thus that they affect his character and those moral actions which are properly so called as representing a character. Any difference which circumstances make to a man, except as affecting the nature of the personal good for which he lives, of the objects which he makes his own, is of a kind with the difference they make to the colour of his skin or the quality of his secretions. He is concerned with it, he cannot live as if it were not, but it is still not part of himself. It is still so far aloof from him that it rests with him, with his character, to determine what its moral bearing on him shall be.[76]

By virtue of his moral freedom, then, man is free to act for good or ill, free to seek self-satisfaction in objects which are virtuous or vicious.[77] In short, his will may be good or bad according to the nature of the objects in which he believes his true good is to be found.[78] Green argues, however, that there is a different sense of 'freedom,' according to which man is really free only to the extent that his will is directed to objects in which he can find true self-satisfaction:

An agent determined by a motive, then, is determined by himself, by that consciousness of himself as the absolute or unconditioned end which makes the motive, and is so far *free*. There is no doubt another and higher sense of moral freedom than that on which we are now dwelling, and which is equally characteristic of the worst act and the best. What we are here describing (to adopt a distinction used by some German writers) may be called *formal* as distinct from *real* freedom. The real or higher freedom is only attained so far as the ends in which self-satisfaction is sought are such as can really satisfy.[79]

The actual nature of those ends in which real self-satisfaction is to be found, that is, the true good, we shall examine in the next chapter. At this stage it is important to establish the meaning of the concept of 'real or higher freedom.'

76 PE, sec. 106; cf. sec. 98. Despite Green's explanations of the effect of character and circumstances on freedom, a number of writers have insisted that he is effectively a determinist. See, for example, A.J. Balfour, *The Foundations of Belief*, pp. 150-1, n.1; C.A. Campbell, *In Defence of Free Will with Other Philosophical Essays* (London: George Allen and Unwin, 1967), pp. 39-40; Henry Sidgwick, *Lectures on the Ethics of T.H. Green, Mr. Herbert Spencer, and J. Martineau* (London: Macmillan, 1902), pp. 15-22.
77 *Hume II*, sec. 4; PE, secs 176, 178
78 *Lectures on Kant*, sec. 118; PE, sec. 154
79 *Lectures on Kant*, sec. 83. (To avoid misunderstanding, I suggest that the last clause of the second sentence of this quotation – 'which is equally characteristic of the worst act and the best' – refers to that sense of freedom 'on which we are now dwelling' and not to 'another and higher sense of moral freedom.') Cf. sec. 117; and 'On the Different Senses of "Freedom,"' *Works*, II, sec. I.

Green's discussion of this concept is highly complex and confusing. It is based upon an assumed parallel with his theory of knowledge. There, it will be recalled, he argues that human knowledge is possible only as a result of the presence of a spiritual principle or eternal mind in man, that this presence makes man conscious of a perfect knowledge, and that man's progressive knowledge of the cosmos of experience is a manifestation of the gradual realization in him of this eternal mind. Similarly, in Green's view, man's moral activity, his attempt to achieve self-satisfaction, is only possible as a result of the presence in him of this spiritual principle; this presence makes man conscious of a moral perfection or true self-satisfaction; and the progressive moralization of man, his struggle to really satisfy himself, is a manifestation of the gradual reproduction in him of this eternal consciousness. Moreover, in the same way as man acquires *true* knowledge only in coming to know the world as it is known by the eternal mind, he can really satisfy himself, can achieve real or higher freedom, only in becoming or striving to become morally perfect through the attainment of ends adequate to a morally perfect being.

This concept of freedom is expressed by Green in terms of the relationship between will and reason. Will, we have seen, is the effort of a self-conscious subject to achieve self-satisfaction; by virtue of his practical reason (his reason or understanding or self-consciousness in its application to the world of practice), man is conscious of moral perfection or true self-satisfaction[80]:

In this most primitive form they are alike modes of that eternal principle of self-objectification which we hold to be reproducing itself in man through the medium of an animal organism, and of which the action is equally necessary to knowledge and to morality. There is thus essentially or in principle an identity between reason and will; and widely as they become divergent in the actual history of men (in the sense that the objects where good is actually sought are often not those where reason, even as in the person seeking them, pronounces that it is to be found), still the true development of man, the only development in which the capabilities of his 'heaven-born' nature can be actualized, lies in the direction of union between the developed will and the developed reason. It consists in so living that the objects in which self-satisfaction is habitually sought contribute to the realization of a true idea of what is best for man – such an idea as our reason would have when it had come to be all which it has the possibility of becoming, and which, as in God, it is.[81]

Real freedom therefore requires 'the reconciliation of will and reason'[82]: 'the good will is the will of which the object coincides with that of practical reason.'[83] How-

---

80 *Lectures on Kant*, sec. 114; 'On the Different Senses of "Freedom,"' *Works*, II, sec. 21; PPO, sec. 6; PE, sec. 177

81 PE, sec. 177. Cf. secs 178, 180; 'On the Different Senses of "Freedom,"' *Works*, II, secs 21, 22, 23, 25.

82 'On the Different Senses of "Freedom,"' *Works*, II, sec. 23

83 Ibid., sec. 22

ever, just as, owing to the fact that the eternal consciousness is reproducing itself in an animal organism, there can be no certainty that in coming to know the system of nature man will not err, that his knowledge of this system may not be incorrect, so there can be no certainty that the will of an individual will conform to his reason, that he will seek his good in objects that will really satisfy him:

We see that in the individual the idea of what is good for him in his actual state of passion and desire – the idea which in fact he seeks to realize in action – is apt not to correspond to his conviction of what is truly good. That conviction is the echo in him of the expression which practical reason has so far given to itself in those institutions, usages, and judgments of society, which contribute to the perfection of life, but his desires and habit are not yet so far conformed to it that he can seek his good in obeying it, that he can will as it directs. He knows the better – knows it, in a sense, even as better for himself, for he can think of himself as desiring what he *does not*, but feels that he *should*, desire – but he prefers the worse. His will, we say, does not answer to his reason.[84]

Furthermore, as we shall see, just as man's existence as an animal organism prevents his acquisition of perfect knowledge, so Green holds that it is impossible for him to fully satisfy himself, to become perfectly free in the higher sense.[85] The moral life of man must be an endless struggle, 'never ending, still beginning,'[86] to achieve moral perfection.

Finally, Green's theory of the reproduction of the eternal self in man is the basis of his teleological view of man and history. In his knowledge, in his morality, and in all spheres of life, Green holds, man is approaching the ideal. In the life of both the individual and the race, man's knowledge is becoming more accurate, his moralization more complete, and his way of life more perfect. More important, however, this view also implies that things are to be seen not only for what they are but also for what they may become. Man especially, because of the consciousness he shares with the eternal subject, should be regarded not merely in terms of what he has so far become and achieved, his 'actual self,' but also in terms of what he is capable of becoming and achieving, his 'possible self.'[87] Indeed, his real, essential self is that which is still to be realized. This view, we shall see, underlies Green's theory of human nature.

84 PE, sec. 179
85 See, for example, PE, sec. 180.
86 'The Philosophy of Aristotle,' *Works*, III, p. 73
87 'The Word is Nigh Thee,' *Works*, III, p. 224. Cf. 'An Estimate of the Value and Influence of Works of Fiction in Modern Times,' *Works*, III, p. 29; 'Faith,' *Works*, III, pp. 269-70; *Lectures on Kant*, sec. 125; *Lectures on Logic*, sec. 17; and PE, sec. 180.

The philosophical foundations of Green's system raise a number of problems. In the first place, Green consistently attacks the classical English tradition from Locke to J.S. Mill for its view of 'man as a bundle of tastes' or appetites.[88] Man, he contends, cannot be understood as the result of solely natural forces but is the vehicle of a non-natural, spiritual principle. Nevertheless, the primary driving force of man's moral activity is appetite or desire. Although for Green these appetites are transformed by reason of their presence to a self-determining subject, man remains fundamentally a desirer of self-satisfaction. If Green did regard man as such an appetitive creature, it is not clear how his system differs, at bottom, from the tradition he criticized.

Second, as we have seen, Green employs two different senses of freedom. To be sure, he was attempting to discard the Kantian opposition between the autonomy and heteronomy of the will[89] by arguing that the will is always free, regardless of its object. But he has introduced his own opposition by maintaining that, although in all acts of will man is morally free, he is not really free unless he wills a particular type of personal good. This difficulty will receive further attention when we look at Green's proposals for legislative reform, where we encounter a third concept of freedom, defined as 'a positive power or capacity of doing or enjoying something worth doing or enjoying.'[90] It is not entirely clear at this point in our study to which (if either) of the first two concepts of freedom the third corresponds, nor whether the antithesis between moral and real freedom has any bearing upon Green's social thought as a whole.

Finally, underlying both of these difficulties, the suspicion persists that, despite all Green's efforts to rid philosophy of its dualisms – feeling vs thought, phenomenon vs noumenon, heteronomy vs autonomy, etc. – his system is itself based upon an essential opposition. The notion of the reproduction of an eternal, divine consciousness in an animal organism seems to have implications which Green did not adequately explore. Man, in fact, seems to represent for Green the focus of all antitheses: it is in man that mind and matter, spirit and body, God and animal, meet and are somehow mysteriously fused. If this dualism does indeed permeate Green's work, it is difficult to understand how such an apparently scrupulous thinker could have overlooked it, since it has serious implications for the whole of his thought.

88 'Popular Philosophy in its Relation to Life,' *Works*, III, p. 122
89 *Lectures on Kant*, secs 89-93, 117-21
90 'Liberal Legislation and Freedom of Contract,' *Works*, III, p. 371

3

The true good or the theory
of self-realization

I

One of the most important, and certainly the most complex, of Green's concepts is
that of the true or ultimate good. Largely contained within the last half of his *Prolegomena to Ethics*, it represents probably his most original contribution to English
social thought, for at the root of his discussion lies his challenge to the liberal view of
man as an infinite consumer of utilities whose *summum bonum* is the greatest possible
pleasure. In its place, we shall see, he argues that the true end of human endeavour,
real freedom, is to be sought in the development of man's uniquely human powers or
capacities.

Usually termed his theory of 'self-realization,' but variously referred to in addition by Green himself as the 'realization of human capacities,' the 'perfection' or
'development' of oneself, and the 'fulfilment of the human vocation,' his concept of
the true good has been, of all his concepts, the least subject to critical examination.
Highly vague and ambiguous at the best of times, Green is no less so here, and the
need for thorough analysis is accordingly no less essential. One may therefore
speculate that the lack of attention to this area of his thought may be due to its
somewhat unusual positioning and expression. Students of Green's political thought
may have considered this area to be outside their field of interest because it is
included in what is for the most part a metaphysical treatise and has no direct
bearing on his theory of political obligation. Students of his epistemology and ethics
on the other hand have by and large not considered the implications of the theory of
self-realization for Green's social and political thought. Nevertheless, since any discussion of the social and political life of man must presuppose a theory of the ends of
human endeavour, a full consideration of Green's concept of the ultimate good is
necessary here.

One recent commentator who has devoted much attention to this aspect of Green's work is Melvin Richter. Placing great emphasis on the religious underpinnings of Green's thought, as we have seen, Richter interpreted the theory of self-realization as, at bottom, a theory of self-sacrifice and 'citizenship.'[1] The true good of man, according to this view, is the subordination of impulse to will, self-denial in favour of dedicated and self-effacing service to one's fellow man.

There is indeed textual evidence to support this view. Although he condemned self-sacrifice for its own sake, Green deemed it virtuous when undertaken 'through interest in the performance of some public duty or other, in the fulfilment of some function or other which falls to us as members of a community.'[2] Moreover, the need for self-denial in the interest of 'self-devotion to an ideal of mutual service'[3] had become an imperative in view of the admission of all individuals to full rights and full membership in the modern state. This placed a burden upon modern man which was unknown to the ancients:

Where the Greek saw a supply of possibly serviceable labour, having no end or function but to be made really serviceable to the privileged few, the Christian citizen sees a multitude of persons, who in their actual present condition may have no advantage over the slaves of an ancient state, but who in undeveloped possibility, and in the claims which arise out of that possibility, are all that he himself is. Seeing this, he finds a necessity laid upon him. It is no time to enjoy the pleasures of eye and ear, of search for knowledge, of friendly intercourse, of applauded speech or writing, while the mass of men whom we call our brethren, and whom we declare to be meant with us for eternal destinies, are left without the chance, which only the help of others can gain for them, of making themselves in act what in possibility we believe them to be.[4]

Nevertheless, the thrust of Green's effort lies elsewhere. The notion of self-sacrifice, for example, must be seen in light of Green's denunciation of pleasure as the object in which true self-satisfaction is to be found. Furthermore, the type of activity he thought should be undertaken in the service of mankind must be more carefully analysed. The notion of self-devoted service is only one element in Green's concept of the true good. It is only part of his concept of self-realization, of the fulfilment of human possibilities and man's development and perfection of his uniquely human capacities.

1 *The Politics of Conscience: T.H. Green and his Age* (London: Weidenfeld and Nicolson, 1964), pp. 254-8, 295-8, 310-30, 344-9
2 PE, sec. 264; cf. sec. 377.
3 PE, sec. 244; cf. sec. 273.
4 PE, sec. 270; cf. secs 264, 271, 273, 275, 280.

2

Green's moral philosophy, we have seen, like his epistemology, depends on an assumed spiritual identity between man and the eternal consciousness. Man is the vehicle in which the divine mind is reproducing itself, the animal being that is gradually becoming the eternal subject. The spiritual principle in man that makes him capable of an ultimate good at the same time makes it impossible for him to find that good in the satisfaction of those desires which result from his animal nature:

It is this that we express by saying that man is subject to a law of his being which prevents him from finding satisfaction in the objects in which under the pressure of his desires it is his natural impulse to seek it. This 'natural impulse' (not strictly 'natural') is itself the result of the operation of the self-realizing principle upon what would otherwise be an animal system, and is modified, no doubt, with endless complexity in the case of any individual by the result of such operation through the ages of human history. But though the natural impulses of the will are thus the work of the self-realizing principle in us, it is not in their gratification that this principle can find the satisfaction which is only to be found in the consciousness of becoming perfect, of realizing what it has it in itself to be.[5]

Accordingly, before proceeding to consider the actual content of Green's concept of the true good, we may from the outset say of it, negatively, that it cannot be found either in the pursuit of pleasure or in material well-being. This assertion follows directly from Green's characterization of man's spiritual nature as eternal, self-conscious, and self-determining.

As eternal, 'we think of ourselves as surviving each particular desire and its gratification.'[6] Because there is a permanent self in us that is present to all the natural sensations we feel, and indeed is the condition of both our knowledge and our moral activity, we cannot find true self-satisfaction in pleasure that is necessarily transitory and hence inadequate to an abiding self. Our true good, in fact, 'is not to be found in the possession of *means* to a succession of pleasures any more than in the succession itself.'[7]

As self-conscious, man is aware of his whole being. That is to say, he is conscious of his various faculties and desires and of their relation to him. Consequently he is unable to find his true good in anything that serves merely to satisfy any one part of

5 'On the Different Senses of "Freedom,"' *Works*, II, sec. 21; cf. secs 1, 23.
6 PE, sec. 230
7 PE, sec. 246; emphasis added. Cf. secs 232, 239, 242; and 'On the Different Senses of "Freedom,"' *Works*, II, sec. 5.

his being, any particular aspect of his existence; pleasure, as particular, cannot satisfy 'the whole man.'[8]

Finally, as self-determining, man cannot find real self-satisfaction in any object not determined through its relation to him because it cannot be adequate to his moral freedom. This assertion is expressed by Green in terms of the opposition between the 'desired' and the 'desirable.' The former is that desire of the subject which itself determines the character of the end or object he pursues as his good; the latter is that desire which is itself determined by its relation to the subject's true good. Strictly speaking, given Green's conception of moral freedom, this opposition is not a valid one. In every desire, Green contends, an individual is necessarily free in the limited sense and is therefore self-determining. However, pleasure, as 'the satisfaction of an animal susceptibility, just as possible without reason,'[9] is in a sense independent of reason and hence independent of man's spiritual nature. Man is capable of seeking pleasure whether or not he shares a community of spirit with the eternal consciousness, so that the search for pleasure is not adequate as his true good.[10]

For Green the ultimate good, the *summum bonum*, lies in the process 'of making a possible self real,'[11] in man's becoming what in promise he is, in his transcendence of his animal nature and his ever-nearer approach to identity with the eternal self.

Through certain *media*, and under certain consequent limitations, but with the constant characteristic of self-consciousness and self-objectification, the one divine mind gradually reproduces itself in the human soul. In virtue of this principle in him man has definite capabilities, the realization of which, since in it alone he can satisfy himself, forms his true good.[12]

'There has arisen, in short, a conception of good things of the soul, as having a value distinct from and independent of the good things of the body, if not as the only things truly good, to which all other goodness is merely relative.'[13]

Moreover, the pursuit of the true good must be actively undertaken. In a sense, all members of the system of nature experience such a process of 'self-realization' in so far as, in the life of both the individual and the species, they develop or evolve into what they potentially or *really* are. Man, however, as a self-determining and self-conscious agent, is related to this process in a fundamentally different way: 'he has the impulse to make himself what he has the possibility of becoming but actually

8 'On the Different Senses of "Freedom,"' *Works*, II, sec. 1; cf. PE, secs 85, 193.
9 *Lectures on Kant*, sec. 128
10 Ibid., sec. 104, addition to sec. 128; 'On the Different Senses of "Freedom,"' *Works*, II, sec. 5
11 'The Word is Nigh Thee,' *Works*, III, p. 224. Cf. *Lectures on Kant*, sec. 128; and PE, secs 187, 199, 286.
12 PE, sec. 180
13 PE, sec. 243

is not, and hence not merely, like the plant or animal, undergoes a process of development, but seeks to and does develop himself.'[14]

To Green knowledge, we have seen, is a process in which man is not merely a passive receiver of sensations but also a creative, constitutive actor. Similarly, man must be an active and creative participant in the achievement of his true good. He cannot, in other words, be a mere collector of pleasures or utilities. The end of human endeavour, therefore, is described by Green 'as a character not a good fortune, as a fulfilment of human capabilities from within not an accession of good things from without, as a *function*, not a *possession*.'[15]

Nevertheless, because of man's sentience, his existence as an animal organism, he tends to seek his good in the satisfaction of his desire for pleasures and material goods. Thus, 'in relation to a nature such as ours, having other impulses than those which draw to the idea, this ideal becomes, in Kant's language, an imperative, and a categorical imperative.'[16] The true good is therefore at the same time a moral good, a good that ought to be pursued because in it alone are we able to find our ultimate satisfaction. Conversely, to suggest that the pursuit of pleasure can provide a moral standard for man is 'absurd':

A merely natural agent cannot present a rule of conduct to itself. The presentation of it, as a rule of what should be done in distinction from what is done, arises from the effort of reason, as a principle of self-realization, conditioning and conditioned by an animal nature, to become what, as so conditioning and conditioned, it is not; the effort to find an end adequate to itself, which it can in truth only find by making it, by giving reality to its own possibilities. The 'good,' the 'desirable' (as distinct from the desired), the 'should be,' the 'moral law,' are different ways of expressing the relation of the self-conscious subject to such an end. So long as reason seeks it in what does not depend on itself, in what it finds but does not make, in pleasure, which is the satisfaction of an animal susceptibility, just as possible without reason (Kant would say, much more possible), it is seeking it in what relatively to it is accidental, in what does not arise out of the principles through which alone there comes to be a 'should be' at all. To say, in short, that I ought to pursue an end, viz. pleasure, which (as those who say it ought to be pursued strongly insist) in virtue of my animal nature I inevitably do pursue, is absurd. Just because the pursuit of pleasure is a physical necessity (though not therefore a necessity to us who are not merely physical), it cannot be morally necessary – cannot be that which *morally* must be.[17]

14 PE, sec. 175. Cf. sec. 352; and 'The Word is Nigh Thee,' *Works*, III, pp. 225-6.
15 PE, sec. 246, emphasis added
16 PE, sec. 196; cf. secs 197, 230.
17 *Lectures on Kant*, sec. 128. See also PE, sec. 171: 'regarding the good generically as that which satisfies desire, but considering the objects we desire to be by no means necessarily pleasures, we shall naturally distinguish the moral good as that which satisfies the desire of a moral agent, or

3

To this point Green's concept of the ultimate good looks fundamentally selfish. His basic premise is the reproduction of the spiritual principle in individuals, and he describes moral activity as the actions of these self-conscious individuals seeking to satisfy their desires. Even his terminology indicates such a view: he speaks of self-satisfaction, of self-realization, of a possible self, of personal ends, and so on. Indeed, Green maintains that 'the moral progress of mankind has no reality except as resulting in the formation of more perfect individual characters'[18]:

The human spirit cannot develop itself according to its idea except in self-conscious subjects, whose possession of the qualities – all implying self-consciousness – that are proper to such a spirit, in measures gradually approximating to the realization of the idea, forms its development. The spiritual progress of mankind is thus an unmeaning phrase, unless it means a progress *of* personal character and *to* personal character.'[19]

It is at first somewhat surprising, then, to learn that for Green the true good must be a common good, a good shared by members of a society. Indeed, scattered throughout his work are no less than four separate justifications of this position.[20]

that in which a moral agent can find the satisfaction of himself which he necessarily seeks. The true good we shall understand in the same way. It is an end in which the effort of a moral agent can really find rest.'

18 'On the Different Senses of "Freedom,"' *Works*, II, sec. 23
19 PE, sec. 185. Cf. secs 182, 183; and 'On the Different Senses of "Freedom,"' *Works*, II, sec. 6.
20 H.A. Prichard, *Moral Obligation and Duty and Interest* (Oxford: Oxford University Press, 1968), argues that the good, for Green, is the satisfaction of the self, and that the common good is therefore an unmeaning concept, 'unless it be maintained that A and B are really the same individual' (p. 125). And, he continues, this is exactly what Green does maintain, i.e. 'where the members of a group of two or more persons are disinterestedly interested in one another's welfare they are really only one person, and not more than one at all ... The self to be made happy is the so-called plurality of selves taken together' (p. 127; see pp. 120-7). Cf. E.F. Carritt, *Morals and Politics* (Oxford: Clarendon Press, 1935), pp. 133-4. In a similar vein, J.H. Plamenatz contends that, because the good must be private, it cannot at the same time be common. *Consent, Freedom and Political Obligation* (London: Oxford University Press, 1938), p. 72. These views, as we shall see, are based on a misreading of Green.
    Dewey, arguing that Green's concept of the true good is not selfish, takes a different approach than that adopted in this study. 'In the ordinary conception of the presupposed self, that self is already there as a fixed fact, even though it be as an eternal self. The only reason for performing any moral act is then *for* this self. Whatever is done, is done for this fixed self. I do not believe it possible to state this theory in a way which does not make action selfish in the bad sense of selfish ... The method with which Green meets the difficulty ... is to split the presupposed self into two parts, one the self so far as realized up to date, the other part the ideal and as yet unrealized self. The realized self acts *for* the ideal self. In so acting, its motive is the ideal self, perfection,

First, Green holds, there is a 'unity of the human spirit throughout its individual manifestations, in virtue of which the realization of its possibilities, though a personal object to each man, is at the same time an object fully attainable by one only in so far as it is attained by the whole human society.'[21] Individual minds in other words share a common origin and a common end by reason of the reproduction in them of the one eternal consciousness, and this 'spiritual principle of social relation'[22] can be traced to the earliest human beings: 'The tendency to form societies, and the reverence for supernatural beings, which even in the darkest days have never been obliterated, are evidences that men were dimly conscious, at once, that their minds were not isolated mechanisms, but pervaded by a life properly the same in every part, and that this life in its turn had its foundations in the life of a higher being.'[23]

Second, because man's spiritual nature is permanent, he demands a good which is permanent, and such a good can only be one that is shared. 'He must in some way identify himself with others in order to conceive himself as the subject of a good which can be opposed to such as passes with his own gratification.'[24] Even 'such an end as provision for the maintenance of a family' Green writes 'implies the thought of a possible permanent satisfaction, and an effort to attain that satisfaction in the satisfaction of others.'[25]

Thus we conclude that, in the earliest stages of human consciousness in which the idea of a true or permanent good could lead any one to call in question the good of an immediately attractive pleasure, it was already an idea of a social good – of a good not private to the man himself, but good for him as a member of a community. We conclude that it must have been so, because it is a man's thought of himself as permanent that gives rise to the idea of such a good, and because the thought of himself as permanent is inseparable from an identification of himself with others, in whose continued life he contemplates himself as living ... But in fact the idea of a true good as for oneself is not an idea of a series of pleasures to be enjoyed by oneself. It is ultimately an idea of satisfaction for a self that abides and contemplates itself as abiding, but which can only so contemplate itself in identification with some sort of society; which can only look forward to a satisfaction of itself as permanent, on condition that it shall

goodness' – and it is therefore not selfish. John Dewey, 'Self-Realization as the Moral Ideal,' *Philosophical Review*, II: No. 6, Whole No. 12 (Nov. 1893), pp. 661-2
21 PE, sec. 377
22 PE, sec. 216
23 'Loyalty,' an early unpublished essay, cited by R.L. Nettleship, 'Memoir,' *Works*, III, p. xxii
24 PE, sec. 246
25 PE, sec. 242

also be a satisfaction of those in community with whom alone it can think of itself as continuing to live.[26]

Third, Green suggests that what he calls 'the social interest'[27] may have developed from animal feelings. 'We may take it, then, as an ultimate fact of human history ... that out of sympathies of animal origin, through their presence in a self-conscious soul, there arise interests of a person in persons.'[28] He is careful to point out, however, that these feelings as they exist in us – like all natural feelings we experience – must have been fundamentally transformed. 'In order to issue in [the social interest] they must have taken a new character, as feelings of one who can and does present to himself a good of himself as an end in distinction from any particular pleasure, and a like good of another or others as included in that end.'[29]

Fourth, just as objects or events in nature have identities – are in fact objects or events – solely in terms of their relations to other objects or events, man's identity is determined by his relations to other individuals. 'Some practical recognition of personality by another, of an "I" by a "Thou" and a "Thou" by an "I," is necessary to any practical consciousness of it, to any consciousness of it as can express itself in act.'[30] Apart from their social relations, Green contends, men are 'imaginary' in the sense that they can have no reality as men for us or for themselves.[31] Man's true personal good can therefore only be a common good:

Now the self, the fuller satisfaction of which is presented as thus absolutely desirable, is from the first a self 'existing in manifold relations to nature and other persons,' and 'these relations form the reality of the self.' Thus the conception of a self to be satisfied necessarily carries with it the conception of this object 'as common to himself with others.'[32]

The true good, accordingly, must be common in the sense of being mutually beneficial, and hence non-exclusive, as well as non-competitive. On the one hand, Green argues, 'the idea [of a true good] does not admit of the distinction between good for self and good for others.'[33] 'Immorality' he writes 'is selfishness, i.e. the

26 PE, sec. 232; cf. secs 231, 240.
27 PE, sec. 200
28 PE, sec. 201
29 PE, sec. 200
30 PE, sec. 190
31 PE, sec. 288. Cf. sec. 183; and 'Popular Philosophy in its Relation to Life,' *Works*, III, pp. 116-17
32 *Lectures on Kant*, addition to sec. 124. It should be noted that this addition, as well as the others referred to, was prepared by Nettleship. It represents an 'outline of the argument' as contained in lecture material which has been omitted. The phrases in quotation marks are Green's own words as cited by Nettleship.
33 PE, sec. 235

direction of a man's dominant interest to an object private to himself, a good in which others cannot share.'[34] Neither pleasure, which by its very nature is particular, nor any good sought by the desiring subject solely for himself – 'the most refined impulses may be selfishly indulged'[35] – can constitute man's ultimate good. On the contrary, 'in all its forms the interest [in a true good] has the common characteristic of being directed to an object which is an object for the individual only so far as he identifies himself with a society, and seeks neither an imagined pleasure nor a succession of pleasures, but a bettering of the life which is at once his and society's.'[36]

On the other hand objects that are particular in their goodness, especially pleasure, are deficient in a further sense:

To be actuated by a desire for pleasure is to be actuated by a desire for some specific pleasure to be enjoyed by oneself. No two or more persons whose desires were only of this kind could really desire anything in common. Under the given institutions of society one man's desire for pleasure may, no doubt, lead to a course of action which will incidentally produce pleasure to another; as in trade, when A's desire for the pleasure to be got by the possession of some article leads him to give B a price for it, which enables B in turn to obtain some pleasure that he desires. But even in this case it is clear not only that desires of A and B, as desires for pleasure, are not directed to a common object, but that, *if left to their natural course, they would lead to conflict*. A desires the pleasure he obtains by buying the article of B, but (*qua desiring pleasure*) he does not desire, he has an aversion to, the loss of means to other pleasures involved in paying a price for it. He only pays the price, and so adjusts his desire for pleasure to B's, because under the given social order he can obtain the article in no other way. The desires, in short, of different men, so far as directed each to some pleasure, are in themselves *tendencies to conflict between man and man*.[37]

The common good, rather, must be 'a good in the effort after which there can be no competition between man and man; of which the pursuit of any individual is an equal service to others and to himself.'[38]

---

34 *Lectures on Kant*, sec. 123; cf. 'The Incarnation,' *Works*, III, p. 219.
35 'On the Different Senses of "Freedom,"' *Works*, II, sec. 23
36 PE, sec. 239; cf. secs 246, 283, 370.
37 PE, sec. 282; emphasis added
38 PE, sec. 283; cf. secs 244, 245, 246. Cacoullos argues that the good, for Green, is non-competitive because he denied the existence of real scarcity. Rather, she contends, he saw the 'ideology of scarcity' as the real villain. Ann R. Cacoullos, *Thomas Hill Green: Philosopher of Rights* (New York: Twayne Publishers, 1974), p. 138, n. 19. This fundamental misinterpretation of Green is based on a misreading of C.B. Macpherson's discussion of Green.

4

Green's true good, we have seen, is 'a function, not a possession'; it satisfies desire, yet is neither pleasure nor material well-being; it is a personal good, yet is a common good both as non-exclusive and non-competitive. Further, it consists in what Green calls 'the perfection of human character,'[39] 'the realization of the powers of the human spirit,'[40] or 'the fulfilment of man's vocation.'[41] But what is the actual content of the ultimate good? What are the powers or capacities of man, and in what type of activity are they to be realized?

As in other matters, Green is not very precise. One searches in vain for a complete, systematic account of his answers to these questions. In this instance, however, there is some justification in his contention that 'no ideal can go more than a certain distance, in the detail of conduct it requires, beyond the conditions of the given age.'[42] Man's vision of his ideal, in other words, is necessarily clouded and distorted by the limitations of his animal nature, as a physical organism existing in time. According to Green, 'we can form no positive conception of what the ultimate perfection of the human spirit would be; what its life would be when all its capabilities were fully realized ... All the notions that we can form of human excellences and virtues are in some way relative to present imperfections.'[43] Nevertheless, an indication of the content of the true good is provided by man's actual accomplishments in his effort to fulfil himself. Green argues 'that from a moral capability which had not realized itself at all nothing could indeed be inferred as to the moral good which can only consist in its full realization; but that the moral capability of man is not in this wholly undeveloped state. To a certain extent it has shown by actual achievement what it has in it to become.'[44]

We have already considered the view that Green's concept of self-realization is of a life consisting in self-denial and devotion to the service of mankind. Given Green's identification of the true good and the moral good, as well as his clear denunciation of pleasure as the ultimate end of human endeavour, this view might also be expressed more broadly as the development of what one might call the strictly moral virtues.

Another possible interpretation of Green's theory is that the true good is to be sought in the perfection of the arts and sciences and of the laws and institutions of

39 See, for example, PE, secs 247, 280, 283, 337, 353.
40 PE, sec. 376; cf. secs 257, 280, 283, 286, 337, 371, 375.
41 See, for example, PE, secs 353, 371, 375, 381.
42 PE, sec. 268
43 PE, sec. 353; cf. secs 193, 196, 239, 337, 352.
44 PE, sec. 172; cf. secs 247, 337.

society, in the development therefore of culture and civilization.[45] Speaking of those human achievements that reveal the possible content of the true good, Green mentions the practical world that has been created 'in the shape of arts, laws, institutions and habits of living, which, so far as they go, exhibit the capabilities of man, define the idea of his end.'[46] In a similar context, he notes: 'We can point indeed to a great realization of human capabilities, which has actually been achieved. Men have been in large measure civilized and moralized; nature has been largely subdued to their use; they have learnt to express themselves in the fine arts.'[47] Consider, finally, the following statement regarding the arts and sciences as necessarily contributory to the common good: 'An artist or man of science,' Green writes, 'who "lives for his work" without troubling himself with philanthropy, is yet not living for an object merely private to himself. His special interest may be shared by no one, but the work which results from it, the machine constructed, the picture painted, the minute step forward in knowledge, i.e. the man's good as attained, is a good for which others are the better.'[48]

45 The view that Green's true good consisted in the development of both the moral virtues and the arts and sciences was adopted by Henry Sidgwick, *Lectures on the Ethics of T.H. Green, Mr. Herbert Spencer, and J. Martineau* (London: Macmillan, 1902). He contended, however, that a good consisting in the development of the arts and sciences could not be non-competitive: 'I think that when we examine in detail Green's conception of a true good for an individual, taking the notion of perfection or complete realization of capacities, we do not find it really so constituted that it cannot possibly come into competition with the true good of any other individual. For this realization of human capacities is repeatedly stated to include "art and science" as well as "specifically moral virtues" ... But if this be so, is it not idle to tell us ... that a man's true good does not consist in objects that admit of being competed for – so long as the material conditions of human existence remain at all the same as they are now? Virtue ... admits of being exercised under any external conditions of life; but the faculties that find expression in the arts and sciences – no' (p. 69). On the contrary, Sidgwick writes, the desire for the realization of such capacities may be seen as 'the main motive of the keen struggle for wealth which educated and refined persons generally feel themselves bound to keep up' (p. 70). 'Why was Aristotle's ideal restricted to a society of free men in the midst of a large group of enslaved human beings? Because only so could the leisure necessary to "realization of capacities" be gained. And is not this largely true of that "realizing the possibilities of the human soul" which Green has in view?' (Pp. 98-9) Thus, he argues, Green 'somehow allowed his thought to swing like a pendulum between a wider and narrower ideal of true good, sometimes expanding it to Culture, sometimes narrowing it to Virtue and the Good Will' (p. 71). Cf. pp. 106-7.
    Commenting on Sidgwick, Cacoullos suggests, incorrectly, that it is not competition itself that in Green's view is incompatible with the common good, but rather unrestricted competition. *Thomas Hill Green*, p. 137.
46 PE, sec. 352
47 PE, sec. 337
48 *Lectures on Kant*, sec. 123; cf. PE, secs 172, 370.

Whereas such an interpretation, like that which equates self-realization with self-sacrifice, is correct if it represents merely one component of the true good, it is misleading if it is identified with the whole of Green's concept. This may be deduced from an example Green employs in the penultimate section of the *Prolegomena*:

As to the particular instance we have been considering, while intrinsic value will not be denied to excellence in music as having a place in the fulfilment of man's vocation, it is a question, so to speak, of spiritual proportion, whether the attainment of such excellence is of importance in any society of men under the given conditions of that society. For, like all excellence in art, it has its value as an element in a whole of spiritual life, to which the moral virtues are essential; which without them would be no realization of the capacities of the human soul. In some Italian principality of the last century, for instance, with its civil life crushed out and its moral energies debased, excellence in music could hardly be accounted of actual and present value at all. Its value would be potential, in so far as the artist's work might survive to become an element in a nobler life elsewhere or at a later time. Under such conditions much occupation with music might imply indifference to claims of the human soul which must be satisfied in order to [make possible] the attainment of a life in which the value of music could be actualized. And under better social conditions there may be claims, arising from the particular position of an individual, which render the pursuit of excellence in music, though it would be the right pursuit for others qualified as he is, a wrong one for him.[49]

Music, or as we shall see any other human capacity, derives its 'value' for Green from its relation to the whole man and, because the true good must be a common good, to the social life in which his capacities are to be realized:

He has other faculties indeed than those which are directly exhibited in the specifically moral virtues – faculties which find their expression not in his dealings with other men, but in the arts and sciences – and the development of these *must* be a *necessary* constituent of any life which he presents to himself as one in which he can find satisfaction. But 'when he sits down in a calm hour' it will not be in *isolation* that the development of any of these faculties will assume the character for him of ultimate good.[50]

It must be a perfecting of *man* – not of any human faculty in abstraction, or of any imaginary individuals in that detachment from social relations in which they would not be men at all. We are therefore justified in holding that it could not be attained in a life of mere scientific or

49 PE, sec. 381. For Richter's interpretation of this passage, see *The Politics of Conscience*, pp. 257-9.
50 PE, sec. 370; emphasis added

artistic activity, any more than in one of 'practical' exertion from which those activities were absent.[51]

Accordingly, neither of the two possible interpretations presented above is adequate in itself to constitute the ultimate good. The type of activity each describes as self-realizing is so only as contributory to a greater good which has yet to be determined.

A brief look at some of the other types of activity mentioned by Green as promoting the true good may provide a clue to its content. 'Such a good' Green holds 'may be pursued in many different forms by persons quite unconscious of any community in their pursuits; by the craftsman or writer, set upon making his work as good as he can without reference to his own glorification; by the father devoted to the education of his family, or the citizen devoted to the service of his state.'[52] The individual may have 'interests ranging, perhaps, from provision for his family to the improvement of the public health or to the production of a system of philosophy ... which, when realized, take their place as permanent contributions to an abiding social good.'[53] Again, Green writes:

No one is eager *enough* to know what is true or make what is beautiful; no one ready *enough* to endure pain and forego pleasure in the service of his fellows; no one impartial *enough* in treating the claims of another exactly as his own. Thus to have more 'intellectual excellence'; to be more brave, temperate and just, in the sense in which any one capable of enquiring what it is to be more perfect would now understand these virtues, is a sufficient object for him to set before himself by way of answer to the question, so far as it concerns him individually; while a state of society in which these virtues shall be more generally attainable and attained, is a sufficient account of the more perfect life considered as a social good.[54]

What, one may well ask, have all of these interests and activities in common? The answer, for Green, is twofold. First, they are all activities, and that, not the accumulation of utilities or pleasures, constitutes the process of self-realization. Second, it is not a certain type of activity that does or does not conform to Green's ideal; what makes a particular activity a constituent element of the true good is the way in which it is done, the spirit that animates it. Thus, Green argues:

that the supreme condition of any progress towards [the] attainment [of human perfection] is the action in men, under some form or other, of an interest in its attainment as a governing interest or will; and that the same interest – not in abstraction from other interests, but *as an*

51 PE, sec. 288
52 PE, sec. 283
53 PE, sec. 234
54 PE, sec. 353

organizing influence upon and among them – must be active in every character which has any share in the perfection spoken of or makes any approach to it.[55]

Green attempts to make this point in his discussion of the different senses of freedom. Of the individual who has not learned to seek his true good, he writes:

His will to arrive at self-satisfaction not being adjusted to the law which determines where this self-satisfaction is to be found, he may be considered in the condition of a bondsman who is carrying out the will of another, not his own. From this bondage he emerges into real freedom, not by overcoming the law of his being, not by getting the better of its necessity, – every fancied effort to do so is but a new exhibition of its necessity, – but by making its fulfilment the object of his will; by seeking the satisfaction of himself in objects in which he believes it *should be* found, and seeking it in them *because* he believes it should be found in them. For the objects so sought, however various otherwise, have *the common characteristic that, because they are sought in such a spirit, in them self-satisfaction is to be found.*[56]

The activity included within Green's vision of the ultimate good is thus not confined to any particular sphere of human endeavour. Indeed, the types of activity he recognized as so contributing have greatly multiplied. 'Faculties, dispositions, occupations, persons, of which a Greek citizen would have taken no account, or taken account only to despise, are now recognized as having their place in the realization of the powers of the human soul, in the due evolution of the spiritual from the animal man.'[57] 'Thus' he maintains 'the ideal of virtue which our consciences acknowledge has come to be the devotion of character and life, *in whatever channel the idiosyncrasy and circumstances of the individual may determine*, to a perfecting of man.'[58] Although a life devoted to selfless service to mankind or the development of the arts may contribute to self-realization, no less so may any other vocation: 'The ordinary activity of men, regulated by law and custom, has its value as contributing to this realization.'[59]

55 PE, sec. 247; emphasis added. Cf. 'On the Different Senses of "Freedom,"' *Works*, II, sec. 21.
56 'On the Different Senses of "Freedom,"' *Works*, II, sec. 1; emphasis in last sentence added. Cf. PE, secs 286, 376; and sec. 110: 'The *prevalent* wish to be better constitutes the being better.'
57 PE, sec. 261
58 PE, sec. 286; emphasis added
59 PE, sec. 337. Cf. Nettleship's somewhat cryptic statement: 'The truth must be (and I am sure this is what [Green] used to teach) that we get to the higher life, not by thinking away the lower, but by carrying it with us; in fact, that the higher *is* the lower, only transfigured or lived at a higher pressure. So that if it were possible to realize fully what one is, or what one is doing, at the most commonplace point of one's life, one would realize eternity – in fact, I suppose, one would be God.' Letter to Mrs Green, July 1882; in R.L. Nettleship, *Philosophical Lectures and Remains of Richard Lewis Nettleship*, ed. with a biographical sketch by A.C. Bradley and G.R. Benson (London: Macmillan, 1897), I, p. 69

This thought is what Green apparently has in mind when he remarks that 'taking human society together, its action in one mode supplements its action in another, and the whole sum of its action forms the motive power of true development.'[60] Although he has argued that the true good must be a common good and that membership in a society is necessary to its attainment, he recognizes that 'this very membership implies confinement in our individual realization of the idea. Each has primarily to fulfil the duties of his station.'[61] Nevertheless, the individual may seek his true good in the fulfilment of such duties, regardless of their actual nature, by seeking his own perfection as a performer of these duties, thereby contributing to the best of his abilities to the common good:

It does not follow from this that all persons must be developed in the same way. The very existence of mankind presupposes the distinction between the sexes; and as there is a necessary difference between their functions, there must be a corresponding difference between the modes in which the personality of men and women is developed. Again, though we must avoid following the example of philosophers who have shown an *a priori* necessity for those class-distinctions of their time which after ages have dispensed with, it would certainly seem as if distinctions of social position and power were necessarily incidental to the development of human personality ...

Thus, under any conditions possible, so far as can be seen, for human society, one man who was the best that his position allowed, would be very different from another who was the best that *his* position allowed.[62]

Returning to the example of the musician beset by social claims upon his activities, we find this point stated in a slightly different manner. Green continues:

In the absence of such claims the main question will be of his particular talent. Has he talent to serve mankind – to contribute to the perfection of the human soul – more as a musician than in any other way? Only if he has will he be justified in making music his main pursuit. If he is not to make it his main pursuit, the question will remain, to what extent he may be justified in indulging his taste for it, either as a refreshment of faculties which are to be mainly used in other pursuits – to be so used, because in them he may best serve mankind in the sense explained – or as enabling him to share in that intrinsically valuable lifting up of the soul which music may afford.[63]

60 PE, sec. 309
61 PE, sec. 183; cf. secs 234, 244, 288.
62 PE, sec. 191
63 PE, sec. 381

In so far as an individual's 'main pursuit' best fulfils his talents and capacities, and hence constitutes his greatest possible contribution to the social good – in other words, in so far as it is carried out with a commitment to perfection, both in himself and in mankind – such activity, regardless of its actual nature, is self-realizing activity.

It is now possible to understand Green's assertion that, in any activity which is to contribute to the realization of his ultimate good, man must be an end, not merely a means. In order for an individual to attain true self-satisfaction, the object of his desire must be, not pleasure or the means to pleasure, but himself as existing in a better state, as realizing his possible self. The spirit which animates his activity, therefore, is the thought of himself as truly fulfilled and of his capacities as fully realized; the end which determines his action is the idea of his own perfection. Only in this way is he truly self-determined, in the sense that he is determined by a conception of his real or possible self. Moreover, since the true good is a common good, those who, as members of his society, are to share in it must also be treated as ends. The individual 'must be able in the contemplation of a possible satisfaction of himself to include the satisfaction of those others, and that a satisfaction of them as ends to themselves and not as means to his pleasure. He must, in short, be capable of conceiving and seeking a permanent well-being in which the permanent well-being of others is included.'[64]

We saw that, owing to man's 'present imperfections,' Green believed it to be impossible to give a full or accurate account of the actual content of the true good. This impossibility had a further meaning for Green, who believed the true good undergoes a continuous process of definition and expansion. As man historically becomes moralized, that is, approaches nearer and nearer to perfection, his idea of that perfection becomes more and more precise and grows richer in the quality of life it prescribes. This, according to Green, involves a twofold process:

Moral development ... is a progress in which the individual's conception of the kind of life that would be implied in his perfection gradually becomes fuller and more determinate; fuller and more determinate both in regard to the range of persons whose participation in the perfect life is thought of as necessary to its attainment by any one, and in regard to the qualities on the part of the individual which it is thought must be exercised in it.[65]

As discussed above, the progressive knowledge of any object or conception is, for Green, its ever-greater concreteness, its ever-closer definition through relation to

---

64 PE, sec. 201; cf. secs 183, 189, 199, 200, 217, 247.
65 PE, sec. 370

the cosmos of experience. Similarly, man's idea of his true good becomes ever more determined through its relation to what he has already achieved, to the world he has created by means of his moral activity. The idea of the ultimate good as a common good has come to be an idea embracing the whole of humanity in a 'universal human fellowship.'[66] Thus, Green maintains, there has developed 'on the one hand an ever-widening conception of the range of persons between whom the common good is common, on the other a conception of the nature of the common good itself, consistent with its being the object of a universal society co-extensive with mankind.'[67] Second, the idea of the possible self to be realized, of the capacities to be perfected, becomes more fully defined:

The idea of the good, according to this view, is an idea, if the expression may be allowed, which gradually creates its own filling. It is not an idea like that of any pleasure, which a man retains from an experience that he has had and would like to have again. It is an idea to which nothing that has happened to us or that we can find in existence corresponds, but which sets us upon causing certain things to happen, upon bringing certain things into existence. Acting in us, to begin with, as a demand which is ignorant of what will satisfy itself it only arrives at a more definite consciousness of its own nature and tendency through reflection on its own creations – on habits and institutions and modes of life which, as a demand not reflected upon, it has brought into being. Moral development then will not be merely progress in the discovery and practice of means to an end which throughout remains the same for the subject of the development. It will imply a progressive determination of the idea of the end itself, as the subject of it, through reflection on that which, under influence of the idea but without adequate reflection upon it, he has done and has become, comes to be more fully aware of what he has it in him to do and to become.[68]

Nevertheless, as noted above, the ultimate good, a state of real freedom, is never fully attainable by man. As a result of his animal nature, as well as the possibility (relative to man) of the infinite determination of the idea of self-perfection, this idea, like perfect knowledge, 'is primarily in man unfilled and unrealized; and within the experience of men it is never fully realized, never acquires a content adequate to its capacity.'[69] The pursuit of the true good consists in 'a life of becom-

66 PE, secs 209, 216
67 PE, sec. 286; cf. secs 206, 271, 273, 280, 283.
68 PE, sec. 241. Cf. secs 257, 261; and 'On the Different Senses of "Freedom,"' Works, II, secs 20, 23. Green, however, warns: 'We must be on our guard against lapsing into the notion that a process ad infinitum, a process not relative to an end, can be a process of development at all.' PE, sec. 189. Although the idea of the true good which he himself holds seems to be just such 'a process ad infinitum,' Green apparently thought that it was relative to an end – but an end that because of our limitations we cannot fully know.
69 PE, sec. 352; cf. sec. 180.

ing, of constant transition from possibility to realization, and from this again to a new possibility.'[70]

The theory of self-realization or the true good as conceived by Green may be summarized as follows:

– Self-realization is not to be found in the pursuit of pleasure or the means to pleasure, nor in the selfish pursuit of any object.
– The true good is a common good in the dual sense of being both non-exclusive and non-competitive. As a corollary of this, it is a permanent good.
– The true good must be sought in the active and creative exertion of human powers or capacities.
– The actual nature of the activity is unimportant as a means of determining whether it is or is not contributory to the ultimate good. It is rather the spirit in which it is performed, the 'state of mind or character'[71] with which it is carried out, that distinguishes it as activity in which man can realize his possible self.
– The major pursuit of the individual must be an activity for which he is best suited, which fully realizes his unique capacities, and which therefore represents his greatest possible contribution to the service of his fellow man. Only in this way is man's personal good at the same time a common good.
– The true good must be a good in which man is an end, and in the pursuit of which all other persons are also treated as ends in themselves, not merely as means to a good in which they have no share.

I shall suggest that Green's theory of self-realization is, in effect, a theory of the mutability of human consciousness, that a change in human consciousness is in fact his goal. However, the full import of this theory cannot be assessed until Green's views on the state and property have been examined.

70 PE, sec. 199
71 PE, sec. 244

4

The state: political obligation
and resistance

I

We have seen that Green's true good is a common good.[1] Variously seen as resulting from the common consciousness shared by all persons, the permanence of the human mind, animal sympathies transformed through their presence to man, or the definition or identification of human personality through relations, the theory of the ultimate good as necessarily a shared good is finally reducible to Green's assumption that man is by nature a social creature. For that reason it is a good which can only be realized in society.

The state, then, as one particular form of society, namely, political society, 'is an institution for the promotion of the common good.'[2] Adopting a predominantly Hegelian concept of the state, Green maintains that the existence of the state implies the prior existence of other societies:

In order to make a state there must have been families of which the members recognized rights in each other ... There must further have been intercourse between families, or between tribes that have grown out of families, of which each in the same sense recognized rights in the other. The recognition of a right being very short of its definition, the admission of a right in each other by two parties, whether individuals, families, or tribes, being very

1 It is important to bear in mind D.G. Ritchie's comment: 'In the ethical writings the phrase "self-satisfaction" or "self-realization" is perhaps the more conspicuous, in the political "common good" (which, however, is used quite as much in the ethical); but it is just because to Green these terms are identical expressions of the end for man that his ethics can escape the reproach of being only the Egoistic Hedonism he professedly rejected come back under a disguised form.' *The Principles of State Interference* (London: Swan Sonnenschein, 2nd ed., 1896), p. 141; cf. p. 144.
2 PPO, sec. 124; cf. secs 118, 121.

different from agreement as to what the right consists in, what it is a right to do or acquire, the rights recognized need definition and reconciliation in a general law. When such a general law has been arrived at, regulating the dealings of members of a family towards each other and the dealings of families or tribes with each other; when it is voluntarily recognized by a community of families or tribes, and maintained by a power strong enough at once to enforce it within the community and to defend the integrity of the community against attacks from without, then the elementary state has been formed.[3]

Indeed, the state is conceived of as a higher level of society:

Thus the citizen's rights, e.g. as a husband or head of a family or a holder of property, though such rights, arising out of other social relations than that of citizen to citizen, existed when as yet there was no state, are yet to the citizen derived from the state, from that more highly developed form of society in which the association of the family and that of possessors who respect each other's possessions are included as in a fuller whole; which secures to the citizen his family rights and his rights as a holder of property, but under conditions and limitations which the membership of the fuller whole – the reconciliation of rights arising out of one sort of social capability with those arising out of another – renders necessary.[4]

The state, in this view, is 'for its members the society of societies, the society in which all their claims upon each other are mutually adjusted.'[5]

The state in other words is that type of society which is best adapted to the full development of both the individual and society – to 'a perfection of individuals which is also that of society, and of society which is also that of individuals.'[6] Unlike previous forms of society, which promoted either the general well-being or the good of self-seeking persons – but not both – the state merges both particular and social interests, so that in endeavouring to realize his true personal good the individual contributes at the same time to the realization of the common good. This merging of interests is described by Green in a minor digression:

When you come to analyze what is involved in the existence of a state, you find that if all interests were identical, there would not be a state. On the other hand, the state tends to

---

3 PPO, sec. 134. Cf. sec. 136; and PE, sec. 286. On Green's view of Hegel's theory of the state, see 'On the Different Senses of "Freedom,"' *Works*, II, secs 4, 5, 6.
4 PPO, sec. 141. On Green's teleological view of history in general, see 'Four Lectures on the English Revolution: Lecture I,' *Works*, III, p. 278; Letter to Henry Scott Holland, 9 Jan. 1869, in *Henry Scott Holland, Memoir and Letters*, ed. by Stephen Paget (London: John Murray, 1921), p. 30; 'The Word is Nigh Thee,' *Works*, III, p. 224; 'Faith,' *Works*, III, p. 270; and PE, sec. 271.
5 PPO, sec. 141
6 PE, sec. 247

overcome and, so far as it approaches perfection, actually overcomes, separation of interests. In other words, just so far as there is a state, interests no longer are merely separate. In the state, separation of interests may be said to exist as one fact of the reality, but as in one sense neutralized by the other fact, which is its opposite, viz. the sense of common interest. Neither would be what it is without the other, but in the state neither retains any separate reality.[7]

In this role the state 'is in tendency or idea ... the reconciler and sustainer of the rights that arise out of the social relations of men.'[8] Through its laws and institutions, that is, the state guarantees those rights or powers the exercise of which is necessary to the realization of the true good, while regulating or limiting the conduct of individuals so far as it tends to infringe upon the ability of others to fulfil themselves. However, it is only because reason is the originator of these laws and institutions – as well as the source of man's obedience to them – that they contribute to this end. 'It is reason which renders the individual capable of self-imposed obedience to the law of his family and of his state, while it is to reason that this law itself owes its existence.'[9]

In conforming to positive law, therefore, the citizen is conforming to the product of his reason – the product of the eternal mind he shares with all other persons. Thus, although such laws may be contrary to his inclinations or impulses, contrary to those ends in which he seeks satisfaction as a result of his animal nature, the citizen in obeying them is directing his will, is making an effort to achieve his personal good in accordance with the dictates of reason, is seeking his good where it may truly be found. 'So to submit' writes Green 'is the first step in true freedom because the first step towards the full exercise of the faculties with which man is endowed.'[10]

To Green the state is an instrument for the moralization of man. The individual, by submitting to the law whether consciously or unconsciously, is seeking his true good; 'the most primitive institutions for the regulation of a society with reference to a common good are already a school for the character which shall be responsive to the moral ideal.'[11]

---

7 *Lectures on Kant*, sec. 62
8 PPO, sec. 142; cf. secs 91, 132, 134.
9 PE, sec. 217. Cf. 'Loyalty,' cited by R.L. Nettleship, 'Memoir,' *Works*, III, p. xxiii; *Lectures on Kant*, sec. 84; 'Faith,' *Works*, III, pp. 269-70; 'On the Different Senses of "Freedom,"' *Works*, II, secs 5, 23; PPO, sec. 251; and PE, secs 180, 203, 205, 216.
10 'Liberal Legislation and Freedom of Contract,' *Works*, III, p. 371. Cf. Letter to Henry Scott Holland, 9 Jan. 1869, in *Henry Scott Holland, Memoir and Letters*, p. 31; 'On the Different Senses of "Freedom,"' *Works*, II, secs 5, 6, 23; PPO, secs 7, 116, 117, 118; and PE, sec. 202
11 PE, sec. 205

Morality and political subjection thus have a common source ... the rational recognition by certain human beings – it may be merely by children of the same parent – of a common well-being which is their well-being, and which they conceive as their well-being whether at any moment any one of them is inclined to it or no, and the embodiment of that recognition in rules by which the inclinations of the individuals are restrained, and a corresponding freedom of action for the attainment of well-being on the whole is secured.[12]

Accordingly, Green rejects the view that the state is the result of a social contract:

It is the radical fault of the theory which finds the origin of political society in compact, that it has to reverse the true process. To account for the possibility of the compact of all with all, it has to assume a society subject to a law of nature, prescribing the freedom and equality of all. But a society governed by such a law as a law of nature, i.e. with no imponent but man's consciousness, would have been one from which political society would have been a decline, one in which there could have been no motive to the establishment of civil government.[13]

The foundation of the state, like that of the other forms of society from which it has developed, is rather the general will, that is, the wills of individuals as directed by reason to the true good, which is by definition a common good. In this way the personal interest of the individual is also general; being willed by each, it is willed for all. This concept, Green argues, is 'the permanently valuable thing in Rousseau'[14]:

He saw that the *moi commun* was the only possible basis for free society, yet the current logic forbade him to regard any such community as other than a kind of invention. Hence his derided doctrine of the Social Pact. Instead of recognizing the *moi commun* as the primary principle, whose operation, however immersed in sense, will alone account for the transformation of animal wants into abiding affections, and thus for the family or any other form of society, he treats it as the result of a contract among 'individual egos,' which yet manifestly presupposes it.[15]

This conviction underlies Green's famous dictum: 'Will, not force, is the basis of the state.'[16] Neither force nor the fear of force can account for political obligation, the 'habitual obedience' rendered by the members of a state to their political supe-

---

12 PPO, sec. 117. Cf. 'The Philosophy of Aristotle,' *Works*, III, p. 58; PPO, secs 6, 18; and PE, secs 286, 321.
13 PPO, sec. 55; cf. sec. 116.
14 PPO, sec. 77
15 'Popular Philosophy in its Relation to Life,' *Works*, III, p. 123; cf. PE, secs 216, 285.
16 PPO, Title, Chapter G

rior. Such obedience must rather be ascribed to the general will, 'that impalpable congeries of the hopes and fears of a people, bound together by common interests and sympathy'[17]:

Thus when it has been ascertained in regard to any people that there is some determinate person or persons to whom, in the last resort, they pay habitual obedience, we may call this person or persons sovereign if we please, but we must not ascribe to him or them the real power which governs the actions and forbearances of the people ... This power is a much more complex and less determinate, or less easily determinable, thing; but a sense of possessing common interests, a desire for common objects on the part of the people, is always the condition of its existence. Let this sense or desire – which may properly be called general will – cease to operate, or let it come into general conflict with the sovereign's commands, and the habitual obedience will cease also.[18]

Force is indeed a necessary adjunct of the sovereign in so far as individuals are swayed by 'particular passions' or inclinations to act against the common interest.[19] However, force should not be its principal feature:

If once the coercive power, which must always be an incident of sovereignty, becomes the characteristic thing about it in its relation to the people governed, this must indicate one of two things; either that the general interest in the maintenance of equal rights has lost its hold on the people, or that the sovereign no longer adequately fulfils its function of maintaining such rights, and thus has lost the support derived from the general sense of interest in supporting it.[20]

A vote of the members of the state is not required to discover the general will. The result of such a vote may or may not coincide with the good of society as a whole, and the decision of a monarch or aristocratic assembly may so coincide.[21] Thus, Green maintains, even the Russian Czar receives the habitual obedience of his subjects because his decrees are, by and large, consistent with the common interest.[22] 'Whatever force may be employed in maintaining custom or law,' he writes, 'however "the interest of the stronger," whether an individual or the few or the majority of some group of people, may be concerned in maintaining it, only some persuasion of its contribution to a recognized common good can yield that sort

17 PPO, sec. 86; cf. PE, sec. 288.
18 PPO, sec. 84. Cf. secs 92, 98; and PE, sec. 283.
19 PPO, sec. 118
20 PPO, sec. 93
21 PPO, secs 98, 99, 118
22 PPO, secs 90, 132

of obedience to it which, equally in the simpler and the more complex stages of society, forms the social bond.'[23]

The problem of political obligation, therefore, is for Green essentially a problem of self-realization. In so far as individuals guided by their reason tend to seek their true good, and in so far as this good necessarily consists in a good that is common, the individual members of society tend to seek their good in a common object, the realization of human capacities. The effort of each individual to attain true self-satisfaction, i.e. his will, so far as he seeks this satisfaction where it is actually to be found, is at the same time a general will – and this general will forms the basis of his habitual obedience to political authority.[24]

We have previously seen that the individual can achieve his true good only through membership in society; this may now be amended to read 'only through membership in *political* society,' for only the state, in fusing personal and general interests by subordinating impulse to a law founded in reason, can give full scope to the possibilities of human endeavour:

To ask why I am to submit to the power of the state, is to ask why I am to allow my life to be regulated by that complex of institutions without which I literally should not have a life to call my own, nor should be able to ask for a justification of what I am called on to do. For that I may have a life which I can call my own, I must not only be conscious of myself and of ends which I present to myself as mine; I must be able to reckon on a certain freedom of action and acquisition for the attainment of those ends, and this can only be secured through common recognition of this freedom on the part of each other by members of a society, as being for a common good. Without this, the very consciousness of having ends of his own and a life which he can direct in a certain way, a life of which he can make something, would remain dormant in a man.[25]

'How, finally,' Green asks, 'can the state be said to exist for the sake of an end, or to fulfil an idea, the contemplation of which, it is admitted, has had little to do with the actions which have had most to do with bringing states into existence?'[26] He

23 PE, sec. 202
24 Cf. PPO, sec. 27, where Green defines 'rational will' as 'the capacity which man possesses of being determined to action by the conception of such a perfection of his being as involves the perfection of a society in which he lives.'
25 PPO, sec. 114; cf. PE, sec. 325. This notion too is implied in Green's assertion that 'social life is to personality what language is to thought. Language presupposes thought as a capacity, but in us the capacity of thought is actualized in language. So human society presupposes persons in capacity – subjects capable each of conceiving himself and the bettering of his life as an end to himself – but it is only in the intercourse of men ... that the capacity is actualized and that we really live as persons.' PE, sec. 183
26 PPO, sec. 124

replies that the end for the sake of which the state exists must have been present to some extent in the minds of the creators of states. 'The pure desire for social good does not indeed operate in human affairs unalloyed by egotistic motives, but on the other hand what we call egotistic motives do not act without direction from an involuntary reference to social good, – "involuntary" in the sense that it is so much a matter of course that the individual does not distinguish it from his ordinary state of mind.'[27] Similarly, he writes:

the proposition advanced is that [an idea of social good] is a determining element in the consciousness of the most selfish men who have been instrumental in the formation or maintenance of states; that only through its influence in directing or controlling their actions could they be so instrumental; and that, though its active presence in their consciousness is due to the institutions, the organization of life, under which they are born and bred, the existence of these institutions is in turn due to the action, under other conditions, of the same idea in the minds of men.[28]

Even the use of force, according to Green, 'has only contributed to the formation of states in so far as its effects have taken a character which did not belong to them as effects of force.'[29]

2

'A power on the part of anyone' Green maintains 'is so recognized by others, as one which should be exercised, when these others regard it as in some way a means to that ideal good of themselves which they alike conceive: and the possessor of the power comes to regard it as a right through consciousness of its being thus recognized as contributory to a good in which he too is interested.'[30] Rights, in Green's view, are those powers of an individual the exercise of which is recognized by other individuals as necessary to the realization of a good in which they all share. Like the obligations imposed by society through its laws and institutions, therefore, rights are justified as tending to promote the true good. Thus, Green contends, 'the claim or right of the individual to have certain powers secured to him by society, and the counter-claim by society to exercise certain powers over the individual, alike rest on

27 PPO, sec. 128
28 PPO, sec. 131; cf. secs 125, 126, 127. For Green's use of historical examples in this context, see PPO, secs 128 and 129 on Napoleon; sec. 130 on Napoleon and Caesar; and 'Four Lectures on the English Revolution: Lecture II,' *Works*, III, p. 309, on Napoleon and Cromwell.
29 PPO, sec. 136
30 PPO, sec. 25; cf. secs 38, 121.

the fact that these powers are necessary to the fulfilment of man's vocation as a moral being.'[31]

By virtue of the reproduction in him of the eternal consciousness, man, we have seen, is capable of the idea of his true good. Unlike the animal or plant, however, which 'may be *made* contributory to social good,'[32] man is able consciously to strive to attain this end. Indeed, it is only in proportion as this end actuates his pursuit of it – that he pursues it freely, as self-determined – that he contributes to its attainment both in himself and others:

The condition of making the animal contributory to human good is that we do not leave him free to determine the exercise of his powers; that we determine them for him; that we use him merely as an instrument; and this means that we do not, because we cannot, endow him with rights. We cannot endow him with rights because there is no conception of a good common to him with us which we can treat as a motive to him to do to us as he would have us do to him.[33]

The capacity of self-perfection, moreover, not only constitutes the foundation of rights but also makes their possession the condition of its realization:

everyone capable of being determined by the conception of a common good as his own ideal good, as that which unconditionally should be (of being in that sense an end to himself), in other words, every moral person, is capable of rights; i.e. of bearing his part in a society in which the free exercise of his powers is secured to each member through the recognition by each of the others as entitled to the same freedom with himself. To say that he is capable of rights, is to say that he ought to have them ... Only through the possession of rights can the power of the individual freely to make a common good his own have reality given to it. Rights are what may be called the negative realization of this power. That is, they realize it in the sense of providing for its free exercise, of securing the treatment of one man by another as equally free with himself, but they do not realize it positively, because their possession does not imply that in any active way the individual makes a common good his own. The possession of them, however, is the condition of this positive realization of the moral capacity, and they ought to be possessed because this end ... ought to be attained.[34]

Although rights, in Green's opinion, predate the state,[35] he is careful to point out that, as founded on a concept of social good, they cannot predate society. 'A right is

31 PPO, sec. 21; cf. secs 20, 26.
32 PPO, sec. 208; emphasis added
33 PPO, sec. 208; cf. secs 27, 139, 154.
34 PPO, sec. 25; cf. sec. 29.
35 PPO, secs 132, 134, 136, 138, 141

a power of acting for his own ends, – for what he conceives to be his good, – secured to an individual by the community, on the supposition that its exercise contributes to the good of the community.'[36] It is therefore the recognition on the part of the members of a society that a particular activity contributes to the social good that renders it a right. 'It is on the relation to a society, to other men recognizing a common good, that the individual's rights depend, as much as the gravity of a body depends on relations to other bodies.'[37]

This notion of 'recognition' is central to Green's theory. Rights, he contends, are 'ideal attributes' of man. Whereas human powers are 'sensibly verifiable,' rights are 'not reducible to any perceivable fact or facts.' 'Nothing is more real than a right,' but only so far as it is recognized by society as somehow related to the common good is the free, unimpeded exercise of a power sanctioned by society, i.e. does it become a right.[38] Thus, Green asserts, 'it is only thinking that makes a might a right, – a certain conception of the might as relative to a social good on the part at once of the person or persons exercising it, and of a society which it affects.'[39]

As a result, Green rejects the view that rights can possibly inhere in individual persons:

There is no harm in saying that they belong to individuals as such, if we understand what we mean by 'individual,' if we mean by it a self-determining subject, conscious of itself as one among other such subjects, and of its relation to them as making it what it is; for then there is no opposition between the attachment of rights to the individuals as such and their derivation from society. They attach to the individual, but only as a member of a society of free agents, as recognizing himself and recognized by others to be such a member, as doing and done by accordingly.[40]

Using the same logic, Green discounts the theory of natural rights. To argue that rights are natural in the sense of having existed in a state of nature, prior to society, is, he suggests, 'a contradiction in terms.'[41]

There is, according to Green, a sense in which rights may be said to be 'natural.' For example, on the basis of this notion of natural rights he defends the rights of slaves:

It is in this sense that a slave has 'natural rights.' They are 'natural' in the sense of being independent of, and in conflict with, the laws of the state in which he lives, but they are not

36 PPO, sec. 208; cf. secs 25, 113, 142
37 PPO, sec. 99
38 PPO, secs 38, 136
39 PPO, sec. 41; cf. secs 26, 136.
40 PPO, sec. 138; cf. sec. 139.
41 *Hume II*, sec. 55; cf. PPO, sec. 31.

independent of social relations. They arise out of the fact that there is a consciousness of objects common to the slave with those among whom he lives, – whether other slaves or the family of his owner, – and that this consciousness constitutes at once a claim on the part of each of those who share it to exercise a free activity conditionally upon his allowing a like activity in the others, and a recognition of this claim by the others through which it is realized. The slave thus derives from his social relations a real right which the law of the state refuses to admit. The law cannot prevent him from acting and being treated, within certain limits, as a member of a society of persons freely seeking a common good. Now that capability of living in a certain limited community with a certain limited number of human beings, which the slave cannot be prevented from exhibiting, is in principle a cabability of living in community with any other human beings, supposing the necessary training to be allowed; and as every such capability constitutes a right, we are entitled to say that the slave has a right to citizenship, to a recognized equality of freedom with any and every one with whom he has to do, and that in refusing him not only his citizenship but the means of training his capability of citizenship, the state is violating a right founded on that common human consciousness which is evinced both by the language which the slave speaks, and by actual social relations subsisting between him and others.[42]

Although rights may therefore not be independent of society, they may be independent of *political* society. 'A man may thus have rights as a member of a family or of human society in any other form, without being a member of a state at all, – rights which remain rights though any particular state or all states refuse to recognize them.'[43] The fact that they have not been recognized by the state does not signify their illegitimacy.

Such rights may accordingly be called 'natural' in the sense that 'they arise out of, and are necessary for the fulfilment of, a moral capacity without which a man would not be a man.'[44] They are natural – not as being prior to society, i.e. not in their origins – but as being necessary to the realization of man's true good, i.e. in the end they serve.[45]

'Natural rights,' so far as there are such things, are themselves relative to the moral end to which perfect law is relative. A law is not good because it enforces 'natural rights,' but because it contributes to the realization of a certain end. We only discover what rights are

42 PPO, sec. 140; cf. secs 143, 144.
43 PPO, sec. 141
44 PPO, sec. 30
45 'A right ... presupposes a capacity judged not from the standpoint of origin but from that of *destiny* – thus making *the basis of rights that which men have in them to become.*' A.P. Leland, *The Educational Theory and Practice of T.H. Green* (New York: Teachers College, Columbia University, 1911), p. 53; cf. John MacCunn, *Six Radical Thinkers* (London: Edward Arnold, 1910), p. 257.

natural by considering what powers must be secured to a man in order to the attainment of this end. *These powers a perfect law will secure to their full extent.* Thus the consideration of what rights are 'natural' (in the only legitimate sense) and the consideration [of] what laws are justifiable form one and the same process, each presupposing a conception of the moral vocation of man.[46]

'There is' Green writes 'a system of rights and obligations which *should be* maintained by law, whether it is so or not.'[47]

Indeed, Green maintains, as the state more nearly approaches what it is in idea, it tends both to increase the number of persons capable of fully realizing themselves and to enhance the possibility of such realization. This it accomplishes through the gradual extension of rights. 'What is the lowest form in which a society is fit to be called political, is hard to say. The political society is more complete as the freedom guaranteed is more complete, both in respect of the persons enjoying it and of the range of possible action and acquisition over which it extends.'[48] In this way the system of rights as actually recognized tends to coincide with the system of rights that ought to be recognized if full scope is to be afforded to the development of human possibilities:

Thus the state, or the sovereign as a characteristic institution of the state, does not create rights, but gives fuller reality to rights already existing. It secures and extends the exercise of powers, which men, influenced in dealing with each other by an idea of common good, had recognized in each other as being capable of direction to that common good, and had already in a certain measure secured to each other in consequence of that recognition. It is not a state unless it does so.[49]

3

A logical implication of Green's theory of rights is that there can be no right 'to act unsocially.'[50] Since all rights derive from society, in the sense that they require social recognition to become 'real,' '[a] right against society as such, a right to act without reference to the needs or good of society, is an impossibility'[51]; for no community could possibly see the granting of such a right as forming an element in its conception of social good:

46 PPO, sec. 20; emphasis added
47 PPO, sec. 9; Green's emphasis. Cf. sec. 27.
48 PPO, sec. 91; cf. sec. 135.
49 PPO, sec. 132
50 PPO, sec. 138
51 PPO, sec. 143

A right is a power claimed and recognized as contributory to a common good. A right against society, in distinction from a right to be treated as a member of society, is a contradiction in terms. No one, therefore, has a right to resist a law or ordinance of government, on the ground that it requires him to do what he does not like, and that he has not agreed to submit to the authority from which it proceeds; and if no one person has such a right, no number of persons have it. If the common interest requires it, no right can be alleged against it.[52]

In general, Green contends, 'so far as the laws anywhere or at any time in force fulfil the idea of a state, there can be no right to disobey them.'[53] But he knows there may be rights that ought to be recognized as rights if the end of the state is to be served. Furthermore, he remarks, 'as actual states at best fulfil but partially their ideal function, we cannot apply this rule to practice. The general principle that the citizen must never act otherwise than as a citizen, does not carry with it an obligation under all conditions to conform to the law of his state, since those laws may be inconsistent with the true end of the state.'[54] Similarly, he writes:

Particular laws may, no doubt, be imposed and enforced by the sovereign, which conflict with the general will; not in the sense that if all the subject people could be got together to vote upon them, a majority would vote against them, – that might or might not be, – but in the sense that they tend to thwart those powers of action, acquisition, and self-development on the part of the members of the society, which there is always a general desire to extend ... and which it is the business of the law to sustain and extend.[55]

Such laws, Green believes, tend to undermine the power of the sovereign by weakening the loyalty of the citizenry, and it is to be hoped 'that this will result in the transfer of sovereignty to other hands before a social disruption ensues; before the general system of law has been so far perverted as to lose its hold on the people.'[56] Thus, 'in a country like ours, with a popular government and settled methods of enacting and repealing laws,' the dissatisfied individual should follow the rule of 'common sense': 'He should do all he can by legal methods to get the command cancelled, but till it is cancelled he should conform to it.'[57]

Nevertheless, Green allows that 'difficulties arise,' especially in instances in which no such peaceful means of change is feasible. To be precise, he enumerates four cases of potential 'difficulty':

52 PPO, sec. 99; cf. secs 141, 142.
53 PPO, sec. 142
54 PPO, sec. 143
55 PPO, sec. 94
56 Ibid.
57 PPO, sec. 100

when either (1) it is a case of disputed sovereignty, and in consequence the legal authority of the supposed command is doubtful; or (2) when the government is so conducted that there are no legal means of obtaining the repeal of a law; or (3) when the whole system of a law and government is so perverted by private interests hostile to the public that there has ceased to be any common interest in maintaining it; or (4) – a more frequent case, – when the authority from which the objectionable command proceeds is so easily separable from that on which the maintenance of social order and the fabric of settled rights depends, that it can be resisted without serious detriment to this order and fabric. In such cases, may there not be a right of resistance based on a 'higher law' than the command of the ostensible sovereign?[58]

On both (3) and (4), Green is totally silent, offering no further clarification of these instances and no reply whatsoever to the question he raises, despite a later reference to the former[59] and his admission that the latter may constitute 'a more frequent case.' Green suggests that (1) usually occurs in the event of 'conflicting powers' co-existing in the same state. Disputes may arise, for example, 'between the constituent powers of a sovereignty, such as king and parliament in England, of which the relation to each other has not become accurately defined, between a falling and a rising sovereign in a period of revolution, between federal and state authorities in a composite state.'[60] What rule, then, is to guide the individual in the decision as to which side to support?

Simply, I should answer, the general rule of looking to the moral good of mankind, to which a necessary means is the organization of the state, which again requires unity of supreme control, in the common interest, over the outward actions of men. The citizen ought to have resisted or obeyed either of the competing authorities, according as by doing so he contributed most to the organization of the state in the sense explained. It must be admitted that without more knowledge and foresight than the individual can be expected to possess, this rule, if he had recognized it, could have afforded him no sure guidance; but this is only to say that there are times of political difficulty in which the line of conduct adopted may have the most important effect, but in which it is very hard to know what is the proper line to take. On the other side must be set the consideration that the man who brings with him the character most free from egotism to the decision even of those questions of conduct, as to which established rules of right and wrong are of no avail, is most sure on the whole to take the line which yields the best results.[61]

58 PPO, sec. 101
59 PPO, sec. 109, question (c)
60 PPO, sec. 103; cf. secs 102, 104, 105.
61 PPO, sec. 106. Cf. sec. 105: 'At the same time, as regards the individual, there is no reason for doubting that the better the motive which determines him to take this side or that, the more he is actuated in doing so by some unselfish desire for human good, the more free he is from egotism, and that conceit or opinionatedness which is a form of egotism, the more good he will do whichever side he adopts.'

More important than cases in which loyalties are so divided that civil war has either already broken out or is on the verge of doing so are those indicated by (2), where the government is despotic. This instance is more fully explained by Green as referring to 'cases where no law, acknowledged or half-acknowledged, written or customary, can be appealed to against a command ... contrary to the public good; where no counter-sovereignty ... can be alleged against that of the imponent of the law; and where at the same time, from the people having no share, direct or indirect, in the government, there is no means of obtaining a repeal of the law by legal means.'[62] In such cases resistance has not yet been actively undertaken, and the dilemma facing the individual is accordingly more difficult.

In the first place, Green argues, the grounds upon which resistance is urged – the right claimed or the law whose repeal is sought – must attract the sympathy of the general populace. In this way the claimed right gains that sense of social recognition necessary to constitute a right:

Thus, just as it is not the exercise of every power, properly claimable as a right, that is a right in the full or explicit sense of being legally established, so it is not every power, of which the exercise would be desirable in an ideal state of things, that is properly claimable as a right. The condition of its being so claimable is that its exercise should be contributory to some social good which the public conscience is capable of appreciating, not necessarily one which in the existing prevalence of private interests can obtain due acknowledgement, but still one of which men in their actions and language show themselves to be aware.[63]

Green continues:

Thus, to the question, Has the individual no rights against enactments founded on imperfect views of social well-being? we may answer, He has no rights against them founded on any right to do as he likes. Whatever counter-rights he has must be founded on a relation to the social well-being, and that a relation of which his fellow-citizens are aware. He must be able to point to some public interest, generally recognized as such, which is involved in the exercise of the power claimed by him as a right.[64]

Violation of the law – even under slavery, on which there was no question of Green's position – cannot be justified unless the 'public conscience' has accepted its illegitimacy.[65] 'The presumption must generally be that resistance to a government is not for the public good when made on grounds which the mass of the people cannot

62 PPO, sec. 107
63 PPO, sec. 143
64 PPO, sec. 144
65 PPO, secs 144, 145, 146

appreciate; and it must be on the presence of a strong and intelligent popular sentiment in favour of resistance that the chance of avoiding anarchy, of replacing the
existing government by another effectual for its purposes, must chiefly depend.'[66]

Green is not insensitive to the special problems of an oppressed people: 'it is
under the worst governments that the public spirit is most crushed; and thus *in
extreme cases* there may be a duty of resistance in the public interest, though there is
no hope of the resistance finding efficient popular support ... Its repeated renewal
and repeated failure may afford the only prospect of ultimately arousing the public
spirit which is necessary for the maintenance of a government in the public
interest.'[67] He therefore suggests that, as in instance (1), 'we can only fall back on
the generalization that the best man – the man most disinterestedly devoted to the
perfecting of humanity, in some form or other, in his own person or that of
others – is more likely to act in a way that is good as measured by its results, those
results again being estimated with reference to an ideal of character.'[68] Green thus
suggests the following 'general questions which the good citizen should ask himself
in contemplating such resistance':

(a) What prospect is there of resistance to the sovereign power leading to a modification of its
character or an improvement in its exercise without its subversion? (b) If it is overthrown, is
the temper of the people such, are the influences on which the general maintenance of social
order and the fabric of recognized rights depend so far separable from it, that its overthrow
will not mean anarchy? (c) If its overthrow does lead to anarchy, is the whole system of law
and government so perverted by private interests hostile to the public that there has ceased to
be any common interest in maintaining it?[69]

Green himself admits the essential futility of his advice. 'Such questions are so
little likely to be impartially considered at a time when resistance to a despotic
government is in contemplation, and, however impartially considered, are so intrinsically difficult to answer, that it may seem absurd to dwell on them.'[70] Moreover, as
in the case of competing powers within one state, although unselfishness and devotion to the common good may give the best chance of choosing the right course of
action, there can be no certainty: 'where the probable effects of a certain line of
action are at the time of taking it very obscure, we cannot be sure that relatively the
best character will lead a man to take the line which turns out best in the result.'[71]

66 PPO, sec. 108
67 PPO, sec. 108; emphasis added
68 PPO, sec. 112
69 PPO, sec. 109
70 PPO, sec. 110
71 PPO, sec. 111

In the final analysis, therefore, Green urges a careful weighing of the alternatives and a conscientious assessment of the merits of the existing government.[72] On the whole, he advises compliance with the law over its violation, obedience to the established sovereign rather than resistance:

As a general rule, no doubt, even bad laws, laws representing the interests of classes or individuals, as opposed to those of the community, should be obeyed. There can be no right to disobey them, even while their repeal is urged on the ground that they violate rights, because the public interest, on which all rights are founded, is more concerned in the general obedience to law than in the exercise of those powers by individuals or classes which the objectionable laws unfairly withhold.[73]

To return again to the example of slavery, Green asserts that, even allowing that the popular support for its abolition is sufficient to justify resistance,

under certain conditions the right of helping the slave may be cancelled by the duty of obeying the prohibitory law. It would be so if the violation of law in the interest of the slave were liable to result in general anarchy, not merely in the sense of the dissolution of this or that form of civil combination, but of the disappearance of the conditions under which any civil combination is possible; for such a destruction of the state would mean a general loss of freedom, a general substitution of force for mutual good-will in men's dealings with each other, that would outweigh the evil of any slavery under such limitations and regulations as an organized state imposes on it.[74]

Green expresses a similar sentiment in the context of his discussion of 'The Right of the State to Punish.'[75] 'An intentional violation of a right must be punished' he argues 'whether the right violated is one that should be a right or no, on the principle that social well-being suffers more from violation of any established right, whatever the nature of the right, than from the establishment as a right of a power which should not be so established.'[76] Indeed, if resistance even against despotic

---

72 PPO, sec. 112
73 PPO, sec. 144
74 PPO, sec. 147
75 PPO, Title, Chapter L. This chapter was published separately in the *Journal of the American Institute of Criminal Law and Criminology*, I: No. 1 (May 1910), as the first paper in a proposed series entitled 'Anglo-American Concepts of Penal Law.'
76 PPO, sec. 189. Later in the same chapter Green makes another revealing statement: 'We may be sure indeed that any ordinary crime – nay, perhaps even that of the "disinterested rebel" – implies the operation of some motive which is morally bad, for though it is not necessarily the worst men who come into conflict with established rights, *it probably never can be the best.*' PPO, sec. 196; emphasis added

governments is to be severely limited, all the more so is it to be avoided where legal possibilities for change exist:

The common good must suffer more from resistance to a law or to the ordinance of a legal authority, than from the individual's conformity to a particular law or ordinance that is bad, until its repeal can be obtained. It is thus the social duty of the individual to conform, and he can have no right, as we have seen, that is against his social duty; no right to anything or to do anything that is not involved in the ability to do his duty.[77]

4

Green's discussion of resistance discloses a basic assumption underlying his political thought about the nature of the ideal state and its system of rights and obligations. Although his objection to the notion of a right of resistance is in itself a logical deduction from his theory of rights, Green's general opposition to political resistance is inconsistent with some of the principles of his thought so far presented.

Because social recognition is required to constitute a right, Green contended, there can be no right against the state, since no society could in the normal course of events be expected to recognize such a right. However, the foundation of rights is the perfecting of man; only so far as they contribute to this end are rights justified. Thus Green is able to maintain that a certain system of rights and obligations ought to be recognized because it would contribute to this end, whereas other rights, such as slavery, should not be recognized.[78]

77 PPO, sec. 100
78 Richter criticizes Green for this inconsistency between rights which have been recognized and rights which should be recognized: 'Nothing could be more certain than that Green would have repudiated any practices substantially at variance with the values of his own society. Yet on the basis of recognition alone, he could not have excluded what he manifestly would have wished to exclude. Nor is this the worst which can be said about Green's theory. For it is simply inconsistent with itself. It is impossible to reconcile the assertion that rights are such only when socially recognized, with the contrary view that there exist rights which ought to be granted, whether or not they are in fact recognized ... When he criticized theories already in the field, he did so on the assumption that his own method alone was valid, and by displaying how impossible it was to apply these other tests. Yet, after developing his own, he proceeds to qualify them until they [have] lost both their original consistency with his system and whatever sharpness of definition they once had.' *The Politics of Conscience: T.H. Green and his Age* (London: Weidenfeld and Nicolson, 1964), pp. 164-5. Unfortunately, Richter can offer no explanation of this inconsistency, except to suggest that it was a result of 'Green's effort to maintain his philosophical position' (p. 164). Nor does he extend his criticism to Green's theory of resistance.
      Despite Richter's contention, it is possible to reconcile these views within the context of Green's theory of rights. There may be rights which are 'natural,' rights which should be recognized but have not been recognized, for the simple reason that the persons upon whose recogni-

Now, Green himself argues that the true good is a moral good, that the individual in other words has a moral obligation to pursue it. Man has, then, upon Green's own showing, a moral obligation or duty to resist political authority in so far as it hinders or prohibits the pursuit of the common good. Green, aware of the possibility of this line of argument, introduces the notion of a 'duty' to resist a despotic government:

I say 'duty' of resistance because, from the point of view here adopted, there can be no 'right,' unless on the ground that it is for the common good, and if so, there is a duty. In writings of the seventeenth and eighteenth centuries, starting with the assumption of natural rights, the question was never put on its proper footing. It was not asked, When, for the sake of the common good, the citizen ought to resist the sovereign? but, What sort of injury to person or property gave him a natural right to resist? Now there is a sense in inquiring upon what sort and amount of provocation from government individuals inevitably will resist ... but there is none in asking what gives them a right to resist, unless we suppose a wrong done to society in their persons; and then it becomes a question not of right merely, but of duty, whether the wrong done is such as to demand resistance. Now when the question is thus put, no one presumably would deny that under certain conditions there might be a duty of resistance to sovereign power.[79]

Green clearly admits, therefore, that the real problem concerns not the *right* but the *duty* of resistance. The right of resistance is not legally a right, but it may in some cases deserve to be recognized as contributory to the ultimate good.[80] Nevertheless, after employing the term 'duty' in two further sections,[81] Green drops it without explanation. No attempt is made to come to terms with the moral dilemma confronting the conscientious citizen when a system of law and government obstructs, rather than assists, the attainment of the common good.

Although allowing that 'in extreme cases' – and no attempt is made to define or specify them – 'there may be a duty of resistance in the public interest,'[82] Green seems generally opposed to resistance. Resistance may sometimes tend to infringe certain rights or impair law and government, but such objections do not mean resistance is never justified. What conditions therefore do justify resistance? To what extent must political authority obstruct the true good before resistance to it becomes a duty? To what extent are means other than open and violent rebellion,

---

tion the 'reality' or legality of the rights depends have not yet been sufficiently moralized. The real problem posed by Green's theory is the one outlined below: what should the individual or class that does recognize these rights do?

79 PPO, sec. 107
80 At one point Green calls it 'ethically' a right. PPO, sec. 27
81 PPO, secs 108, 109
82 PPO, sec. 108

such as civil disobedience, justified? These are significant issues, but Green remains silent on them. Nevertheless, upon Green's own principles, an equal case can be made for both positions. Furthermore, Green's moral principles demand that the problem be dealt with fully and honestly.

The inconsistency is further clarified by two specific positions Green felt compelled to adopt. He condemned slavery, but he was very cautious in describing the conditions under which its practice might be cause for resistance to established authority. Only when sufficient popular support exists, he argues, can it afford a justification for social disruption, and even then only so far as this disruption does not 'result in general anarchy.' This position was taken by Green some seventy years after the abolition of the English slave trade, and over forty years after the abolition of slavery in the British West Indies. The inhumanity of the slave trade was a matter of public record. There was no foundation for Green's warning that 'such a destruction of the state,' which might be precipitated by resistance to slavery, 'would mean a general loss of freedom ... that would outweigh the evil of slavery *under such limitations and regulations as an organized state imposes on it.*'[83] Green's moral principles, which could not justify slavery, were compromised.

Second despite the obviously democratic character of his thought,[84] Green opposed most attempts at resistance against despotic governments. Since even goodness of character could not ultimately ensure the correctness of one's decision whether or not to resist, Green's presumption was in favour of the *status quo*. He closes his discussion of resistance against despotism with the following comments:

In regard to the questions stated above as those which the good citizen should set himself in contemplation of a possible rebellion,[85] though they are questions to which it is impossible for a citizen in the heat of a revolutionary crisis to give a sufficient answer, and which in fact can only be answered after the event, yet they represent objects which the good citizen will set before himself at such times; and in proportion to the amount of good citizenship, as measured by interest in those objects, interest in making the best of *existing* institutions, in *maintaining* social order and the general fabric of rights, interest which leads to a *bona fide* estimate of the value of the *existing* government in its relation to public good, will be the good result of the political movement.[86]

83 PPO, sec. 147; emphasis added
84 See James Bryce, *Studies in Contemporary Biography* (London: Macmillan, 1903), pp. 87-8; Edward Caird, Preface to *Essays in Philosophical Criticism*, ed. by Andrew Seth and R.B. Haldane (New York: Burt Franklin, 1971; originally published, 1883), pp. 4-5; and John Addington Symonds, *The Letters of John Addington Symonds*, 3 vols, ed. Herbert M. Schueller and Robert L. Peters (Detroit: Wayne State University Press, 1968-9), III, pp. 176-7.
85 PPO, sec. 109
86 PPO, sec. 112; emphasis added

Green's overriding concern in discussing resistance is not the perfecting of man but political stability. He chose to compromise his moral standards rather than to vindicate them through a forthright condemnation of slavery and despotism and through bold support of the duty of resistance where such a duty clearly exists.[87]

What led Green to give precedence to stability over self-development? The England of Green's time was of course a highly volatile society, and the threat of revolution was clearly present; Green rejected outright any resistance in England, where legal channels for change were available. Perhaps Green's preoccupation with social order was his own testimony to the uneasiness and uncertainty of his times. It was not the institution of slavery nor the rule of despots that he sought to protect, but the order and stability of his own England. Green's wholesale opposition to resistance, in short, arose from the fear felt by himself and his contemporaries at the possibility of the dissolution of English society, and this fear concealed from him the fact that his position was essentially untenable.

On a more fundamental level, Green's concern with social order reveals an assumption implicit in his social and political thought as a whole. Political stability for Green is not an end-in-itself but is valuable only as tending to maintain the institutions necessary for the realization of the ultimate good. Green did not view the major institutions of English society as posing an obstacle to the perfecting of man; on the contrary, he believed them to be especially suited to this task. As we have seen, he thought that 'so far as the laws anywhere or at any time in force fulfil the

87 Ernest Barker, who saw the possible inconsistency in Green's position, gave the following explanation, which does not come to terms with the real problem, but probably represents what Green himself might have said: 'These natural rights may be recognized by the general social conscience of such a society, and yet not be recognized by its laws: they may, indeed, only be recognized by those, perhaps the merest minority, who claim their possession. How far do they warrant resistance to the actual law of the community which embodies the rights it has actually recognized? How far, for instance, could a sympathizer with the cause of the negro slave resist the master's legal right of property over the slave in the name of the natural right of the slave to be a free man? In order to give an answer to this question we must distinguish between a natural right already implicitly acknowledged by social conscience, and a natural right not thus acknowledged; and we may concede to the former what we can hardly concede to the latter. The reason for the distinction is plain. The natural right is indeed a necessary condition of a full general welfare, which can only be attained through the liberation of the capacity of every possible contributor; but the whole system of rights already legally acknowledged is also such a condition, or rather it is a whole set of such conditions. Here we see the need for obedience to the rule of law. We must not sacrifice what is almost the whole for the sake of a part; we must not risk social chaos, and the disturbance of the existing system of rights, for the sake of adding a new element to the system. But when there is already an implicit social acknowledgement of the claim to a natural right, we know that there is no possibility of such sacrifice or such risk.' Sir Ernest Barker, *Political Thought in England: 1848 to 1914*, 2d ed. (London: Oxford University Press, 1947), pp. 31-2

idea of a state, there can be no right to disobey them.'[88] Thus, Green's society, along with its system of rights and obligations, apparently represented to him the ideal state in process of becoming. Neither resistance to the English government nor violation of its laws could be tolerated.

In particular, I suggest that for Green, as for those liberal thinkers who preceded or followed him, political stability made possible the smooth and efficient operation of the market system. Thus, the preference given to stability over self-perfection in Green's political thought – like the preference for security over equality in Bentham's thought – reflects his conviction that the capitalist market economy is a necessary fixture of the ideal state and therefore a prerequisite for the realization of the true good. The nature and extent of this conviction form the subject of the next chapter.

5

Property and social classes

Green's examination of property rights is not an exhaustive discussion of the subject, nor was it so intended. His immediate concern was to propose a means of alleviating the miserable condition of the lower classes, and of the 'proletariate' in particular. He argued that that could best be accomplished through remedial legislation. The liberal tradition, he believed, was not adequate to the task at hand. Although it had in the past successfully championed private property and the market economy, it had led 'in the sacred name of individual liberty,'[1] to a general policy of 'laissez-faire,' of resistance to such 'positive reforms' as had under the circumstances become necessary.[2] However, the inability of classical liberal theory to meet the needs of his society was in his view evidence not of the inadequacies of the market system, but of the failure of that theory. On a broader scale, therefore, Green's purpose was to demonstrate that the free market system was not in itself responsible for the prevailing difficulties. On the contrary, this system was essential to the perfecting of man, and such measures as were instituted would have to be compatible with its basic principles. Moreover, implicit in his analysis is a theory of social classes based on the notion of a consciousness shared by their members with a classless society as the social ideal.

I

Green begins his formal consideration of the rights of property by asking 'how men have come to appropriate,' that is, what moves them to appropriate and to what end do they acquire possessions?[3] This question in his view cannot be answered by the

---

1 'Liberal Legislation and Freedom of Contract,' *Works*, III, p. 367
2 PPO, sec. 18
3 PPO, sec. 211; cf. sec. 212.

liberal concept of appropriation as supplying pleasures and the means of life. 'Appropriation' he writes 'is an expression of will; of the individual's effort to give reality to a conception of his own good ... It is different from mere provision to supply a future want.'[4] The acquisition of permanent possessions implies that man is other and more than a merely sentient organism, that by sharing a community of mind with the eternal consciousness he is self-conscious:

acts of appropriation ... are not merely a passing employment of such materials as can be laid hands on to satisfy this or that want, present or future, felt or imagined, but reflect the consciousness of a subject which distinguishes itself from its wants; which presents itself to itself as still there and demanding satisfaction when this or that want, or any number of wants, have been satisfied; which thus not merely uses a thing to fill a want, and in so doing at once destroys the thing and for the time removes the want, but says to itself, 'This shall be mine to do as I like with, to satisfy my wants and express my emotions as they arise.'[5]

Man therefore appropriates in order to satisfy his physical – but uniquely human – desires. However, in virtue of his spiritual nature, as we have seen, he is capable of conceiving the true good and of shaping his actions in accordance with this conception; he has 'personality in the ethical sense.'[6] In proportion as man's will is directed by his reason, i.e. has become rational, to the extent that his actions and acquisitions are determined by his conception of the true good, his possessions constitute as well the means of self-realization or self-expression – 'a permanent apparatus for carrying out a plan of life, for expressing ideas of what is beautiful, or giving effect to benevolent wishes.'[7]

While this may explain the origin of possessions among men, it is also necessary to consider 'how the idea of right has come to be associated with their appropriations.'[8] Here again, Green departs from the liberal individualist notion of property, arguing that property, like all rights, has a 'social character' because it originates in the social recognition of its contribution to the general well-being. Only in so far as powers or claimed rights receive social recognition do they become 'real' or legal rights. Similarly, property implies, for Green, 'the recognition by others of a man's appropriations as something which they will treat as his, not theirs, and the guaran-

4 PPO, sec. 213
5 PPO, sec. 213; cf. secs 214, 217.
6 PPO, sec. 25; also referred to by Green as the 'moral personality' or 'moral capacity.' Cf. PPO, secs 26, 27, 154, 208; PE, secs 182, 183, 190.
7 PPO, sec. 220. Cf. secs 213 ('to satisfy my wants and express my emotions'), 214 ('instruments of satisfaction and expression'), 215 ('for the maintenance and expression of that life'), and 220 ('the ethical purposes which the possession of property should serve').
8 PPO, sec. 211

tee to him of his appropriations by means of that recognition.'⁹ This recognition was overlooked by such writers as Grotius and Hobbes, whereas Locke, while so far correct in discerning a connection between the foundation of property and that of the right to life, added nothing of substance to the discussion. 'The ground of recognition is the same in both cases, and it is Locke's merit to have pointed this out; but what the ground is he does not consider, shelving the question by appealing to a law of nature and reason.'¹⁰

Green justifies the right to life and liberty, or, as he prefers, the right to 'free life' – 'for there can be no right to mere life, no right to life on the part of a being that has not also the right to use the life according to the motions of its own will'¹¹ – on the ground that man is a self-determining agent. This self-determination, we have seen, constitutes man's moral freedom and is the precondition of both his conception of the true good and the possibility of his achieving it. 'Prevent a man from possessing property (in the ordinary sense), and his personality may still remain. Prevent him (if it were possible) from using his body to express a will, and the will itself could not become a reality; he would not be really a person.'¹²

The social recognition that the true personal good is a common good attainable only through a free life renders such a life a right.¹³ That recognition furthermore 'constitutes the right to the instruments of such life, making each regard the possession of them by the other as for the common good.'¹⁴ The right to free life, Green maintains, 'carries with it a certain right to property, to a certain permanent apparatus beyond the bodily organs, for the maintenance and expression of that life.'¹⁵ Indeed, he seems to suggest that an individual's appropriations become a part of his personality. Man's possessions, which 'he takes and fashions,' 'cease to be external things. They become a sort of extension of the man's organs, the constant apparatus through which he gives reality to his ideas and wishes.'¹⁶

9 PPO, sec. 214
10 PPO, sec. 215
11 PPO, sec. 151
12 PPO, sec. 150
13 PPO, secs 150, 151, 154
14 PPO, sec. 216
15 PPO, sec. 215. Cf. sec. 114: 'For that I may have a life which I can call my own, I must not only be conscious of myself and of ends which I present to myself as mine; I must be able to reckon on a certain freedom of action and acquisition for the attainment of those ends ... Without this, the very consciousness of having ends of his own and a life which he can direct in a certain way, a life of which he can make something, would remain dormant in man.' Cf. PE, sec. 191.
    The association between 'action' and 'acquisition' is a recurrent theme in Green's *Principles of Political Obligation*. See, for example, secs 91, 105, 114, 185, 186, 204; 'action, acquisition and self-development,' secs 94, 108.
16 PPO, sec. 215

Property, then, is grounded in the recognition by the members of a society that 'every one has an interest in securing to every one else the free use and enjoyment and disposal of his possessions, so long as that freedom on the part of one does not interfere with a like freedom on the part of others,'[17] that property is necessary to the realization of will and therefore to the possibility of the ultimate good.

Thus the doctrine that the foundation of the rights of property lies in the will, that property is 'realized will,' is true enough if we attach a certain meaning to 'will'; if we understand by it, not the momentary spring of any and every spontaneous action, but a constant principle, operative in all men qualified for any form of society, however frequently overborne by passing impulses, in virtue of which each seeks to give reality to the conception of a well-being which he necessarily regards as common to himself with others. A will of this kind explains at once the effort to appropriate, and the restraint placed on each in his appropriations by a customary recognition of the interest each has in the success of the like effort on the part of the other members of a society with which he shares a common well-being.[18]

A further implication Green draws from the notion of self-determination is that individuals will contribute most to the common good in proportion as their activities are unrestrained by external influences. Although a certain amount of restriction is unavoidable in any human society, the perfecting of man thus requires as little limitation as possible of his powers of appropriation. Green develops this point in the context of a brief digression into the historical origins of property, tracing it back to the family:

We are apt indeed to think of the state of things in which the members of a family or clan hold land and stock in common, as the antithesis of one in which rights of property exist. In truth it is the earliest stage of their existence, because the most primitive form of society in which the fruit of his labour is secured to the individual by the society, under the influence of the conception of a common well-being. The characteristic of primitive communities is not the absence of distinction between 'meum' and 'tuum,' *without which no society of intelligent as opposed to instinctive agents would be possible at all*, but the common possession of certain materials, in particular land, on which labour may be expended.[19]

However, the powers and rights of possession as established in the family are in Green's view inadequate for full human development:

17 'Liberal Legislation,' *Works*, III, p. 372; cf. PE, sec. 210.
18 PPO, sec. 217; cf. sec. 221.
19 PPO, sec. 218; emphasis added. On property rights prior to the state, see also sec. 141 and PE, sec. 216.

A necessary condition at once of the growth of a free morality, i.e. a certain behaviour of men determined by an understanding of moral relations and by the value which they set on them as understood, and of the conception of those relations as relations between all men, is that *free play* should be given to every man's powers of appropriation. Moral freedom is not the same thing as a control over the outward circumstances and appliances of life. It is the end to which such control is a generally necessary means, and which gives it its value. In order to obtain this control, men must cease to be limited in their activities by the customs of the clan. The *range* of their appropriations must be extended; they must include more of the *permanent material* on which labour may be expended, and not merely the passing products of labour spent on unappropriated material.[20]

Whether or not the individual actually pursues the ultimate good, the very possibility of its attainment by him is contingent upon this 'free play' being afforded to his powers of appropriation.

The rationale of property, as we have seen, is that everyone should be secured by society in the power of getting and keeping the means of realizing a will, which in possibility is a will directed to social good. Whether anyone's will is actually and positively so directed, does not affect his claim to the power. This power should be secured to the individual irrespectively of the use which he actually makes of it, so long as he does not use it in a way that interferes with the exercise of like power by another, on the ground that its *uncontrolled* exercise is the condition of attainment by man of that free morality which is his highest good.[21]

The premise implicit in this line of reasoning is that a market economy, in which the acquisitive powers of all are allowed unrestricted 'free play,' is essential to the realization of the true good. However, Green leaps from this to the notion – based apparently on the assumption that man is by nature not merely an appropriator but an infinite appropriator – that, given 'the unchecked freedom of appropriation,'[22] individuals will appropriate without limit. Moreover, as indicated by references to the 'unlimited accumulation of wealth'[23] and the 'unlimited accumulation of capi-

20 PPO, sec. 219; emphasis added. Cf. secs 216 ('a common interest in the free play of the powers of all'), and 220 ('the emancipation of the individual and the free play given to the powers of appropriation'); and 'Liberal Legislation,' *Works*, III, p. 379: 'It is agreed that as a general rule the more freedom of contract we have the better, with a view to that more positive freedom which consists in an *open field* for all men to make the best of themselves.' Emphasis added
21 PPO, sec. 221; emphasis added
22 PPO, sec. 222. Green's assumption that man is an infinite appropriator will be dealt with at greater length in the next chapter.
23 PPO, sec. 226

tal,'[24] Green considers such unlimited individual appropriation to be a right, despite the inequality which is its inevitable result:

Once admit as the idea of property that nature should be progressively adapted to the service of man by a process in which each, while working freely or for himself, i.e. as determined by a conception of his own good, at the same time contributes to the social good, and it will follow that property must be unequal. If we leave a man free to realize the conception of a possible well-being, it is impossible to limit the effect upon him of his desire to provide for his future well-being, as including that of the persons in whom he is interested, or the success with which at the prompting of that desire he turns resources of nature to account.[25]

Indeed, Green fully acknowledges that the practices entailed by his theory of property produce inequality, 'for the theory logically necessitates freedom both in trading and in the disposition of his property by the owner, so long as he does not interfere with the like freedom on the part of others.'[26] As to the former, the term 'freedom of trade' 'may no doubt be used to cover objectionable transactions, in which advantage is taken of the position of sellers who from circumstances are not properly free to make a bargain.' Such is the case, for example, 'when the cheapness of buying arises from the presence of labourers who have no alternative but to work for "starvation wages."' Nevertheless, by bringing commodities from 'where they are of least use' to 'where they are of most use,' this freedom is beneficial to society as a whole. 'The trader who profits by the transaction is profiting by what is at the same time a contribution to social well-being.'[27] Accordingly, this freedom must be guaranteed to the individual in spite of the inequality it causes.

Freedom of bequest, Green maintains, must be similarly guaranteed. 'The same principle which forbids us to limit the degree to which a man may provide for his future, forbids us to limit the degree to which a man may provide for his children, these being included in his forecast of his future.' However, the accumulation of wealth is not a result of inheritance as such; if an estate is divided equally among an individual's heirs, 'the accumulation will be checked. It is not therefore the right of inheritance, but the right of bequest, that is most likely to lead to accumulation of wealth, and that has most seriously been questioned by those who hold that universal ownership is a condition of moral well-being.'[28] Nonetheless, 'if the sense of family responsibility is to have free play, the man must have due control over his

24 PPO, sec. 228. Cf. secs 229 ('unlimited acquisition of wealth') and 230 ('unlimited individual ownership').
25 PPO, sec. 223; cf. sec. 224.
26 PPO, sec. 222
27 PPO, sec. 224
28 Ibid.

family, and this he can scarcely have if all his children as a matter of necessity inherit equally, however undutiful or idle or extravagant they may be.' In this way, 'the father of a family, if left to himself ... is most likely to make that distribution among his children which is most for the public good.'[29]

In addition, Green argues, inequality may be attributed to the differences in the natural capacities of individuals and the variety of vocations through which they accordingly endeavour to realize themselves:

The very existence of mankind presupposes the distinction between the sexes; and as there is a necessary difference between their functions, there must be a corresponding difference between the modes in which the personality of men and women is developed. Again, though we must avoid following the example of philosophers who have shown an *a priori* necessity for those class-distinctions of their time which after ages have dispensed with, it would certainly seem as if distinctions of social position and power were necessarily incidental to the development of human personality. *There cannot be this development without a recognized power of appropriating material things.* This appropriation must vary in its effects according to talent and opportunity, and from that variation again must result differences in the form which personality takes in different men.[30]

'The artist and man of letters' he writes 'require different equipment and apparatus from the tiller of land and the smith'[31]; but the only alternative to inequality is unacceptable, because it is inconsistent with self-determination. 'Either then the various apparatus needed for various functions must be provided for individuals by society, which would imply a complete regulation of life incompatible with that highest object of human attainment, a free morality; or we must trust for its provision to individual effort, which will imply inequality between the property of different persons.'[32]

There has, however, been created a class of persons for all practical purposes deprived of property rights:

29 PPO, sec. 225. 'The main point about this argument for us is its astonishing irrelevance to problems that had been so much accentuated by the industrial revolution. What we want to know is the fate of the masses whose parents have no property to bestow upon them.' H.D. Lewis, 'Individualism and Collectivism: A Study of T.H. Green,' in his *Freedom and History* (London: George Allen and Unwin, 1962), p. 74
30 PE, sec. 191; emphasis in penultimate sentence added
31 PPO, sec. 223
32 Ibid. There is no basis, as far as I can see, for Vincent Knapp's contention that 'what [Green] obviously wanted to see was property more widely diffused in the society.' *Agora*, I: No. 1 (Fall 1969), p. 63. This notion is attacked by John MacCunn, *Six Radical Thinkers* (London: Edward Arnold, 1910), p. 263.

the actual result of the development of rights of property in Europe, as part of its general political development, has so far been a state of things in which all indeed *may* have property, but great numbers in fact cannot have it ... In the eye of the law they have rights of appropriation, but in fact they have not the chance of providing means for a free moral life, of developing and giving reality or expression to a good will, an interest in social well-being. A man who possesses nothing but his powers of labour and who has to sell these to a capitalist for bare daily maintenance, might as well, in respect of the ethical purposes which the possession of property should serve, be denied rights of property altogether.[33]

Moreover, as already noted, the property to which Green here refers is 'a permanent apparatus for carrying out a plan of life,'[34] 'the permanent material on which labour may be expended,'[35] in other words, the means of labour.

Clearly, upon Green's own principles, if the proletariat were the result of the inequities necessitated by the free play of the powers of individual appropriation – by the operation of the capitalist market economy – his theory of property could not be justified. 'In that case' he asserts 'it may truly be said that "property is theft."'[36] But such an assessment of the effects of private appropriation, he contends, is incorrect. Rather than reducing the possibility of ownership by members of the class of labourers, the system of private appropriation actually enhances it by creating new sources of income and wealth both for the proletariat and for society as a whole:

the increased wealth of one man does not naturally mean the diminished wealth of another. We must not think of wealth as a given stock of commodities of which a larger share cannot fall to one without taking from the share that falls to another. The wealth of the world is constantly increasing in proportion as the constant production of new wealth by labour exceeds the constant consumption of what is already produced ... Therefore in the accumulation of wealth ... there is nothing which tends to lessen for anyone else the possibilities of ownership. On the contrary, supposing trade and labour to be free, wealth must be constantly distributed throughout the process in the shape of wages to labourers and of profits to those who mediate in the business of exchange.[37]

Thus, although the free market system does entail a certain economic inequality, Green does not attribute to this system the creation of a propertyless class. 'It is not then to the accumulation of capital, but to the condition, due to antecedent circumstances unconnected with that accumulation, of the men with whom the capitalist

33 PPO, sec. 220
34 Ibid.
35 PPO, sec. 219. Cf. secs 221 and 222 ('such ownership as is needed to moralize a man').
36 PPO, sec. 221. Cf. sec. 222; and PE, secs 270, 273, 274.
37 PPO, sec. 226. Elsewhere, Green contradicts the argument of this passage: see p. 106, note 54.

deals and whose labour he buys on the cheapest terms, that we must ascribe the multiplication in recent times of an impoverished and reckless proletariate.'[38]

Green traces the existence of the proletariat to the fact that 'the appropriation of land by individuals has in most countries ... been originally effected, not by the expenditure of labour or the results of labour on the land, but by force. The original landlords have been conquerors.'[39] This fact does not for Green invalidate either the property rights of current possessors or his theory of property in general. As he argued regarding the formation of states, selfish motives arising from man's animal nature may have acted in conjunction with the spiritual principle in him to produce certain present characteristics of the institution of property incompatible with its idea. 'Still, without that principle, it could not have come into existence, nor would it have any moral justification at all.'[40]

The original conquest of the land, however, has in two ways tended to produce a proletariat. First, members of the working class were 'men whose ancestors, if not themselves, were trained in habits of serfdom' and who for this reason were 'in no condition to contract freely for the sale of their labour, and had nothing of that sense of family-responsibility which might have made them insist on having the chance of saving. Landless countrymen, whose ancestors were serfs, are the parents of the proletariate of great towns.'[41]

Second, Green maintains, 'rights have been allowed to landlords, incompatible with the true principle on which rights of property rest, and tending to interfere with the development of the proprietorial capacity in others.' This tendency has been especially harmful owing to the nature of land as a limited essential resource:

The only justification for this appropriation, as for any other, is that it contributes on the whole to social well-being; that the earth as appropriated by individuals under certain conditions becomes more serviceable to society as a whole, including those who are not proprietors of the soil, than if it were held in common. The justification disappears if these conditions are not observed; and from government having been chiefly in the hands of appropriators of the soil, they have been allowed to 'do what they would with their own,' as if land were merely like so much capital, admitting of indefinite extension.[42]

As a result, individuals have been 'extruded from the soil'[43] without an alternative means of livelihood. 'Thus the whole history of the ownership of land in Europe has

38 PPO, sec. 227
39 PPO, sec. 228; cf. sec. 230.
40 PPO, sec. 217
41 PPO, sec. 229
42 Ibid.
43 Ibid.

been of a kind to lead to the agglomeration of a proletariate, neither holding nor *seeking* property, wherever a sudden demand has arisen for labour in mines and manufactures.'[44] Moreover:

while those influences of feudalism and landlordism which tend to throw a shiftless population upon the centres of industry have been left unchecked, nothing till quite lately was done to give such a population a chance of bettering itself, when it had been brought together. Their health, housing, and schooling were unprovided for. They were left to be freely victimized by deleterious employments, foul air, and consequent craving for deleterious drinks. When we consider all this, we shall see the unfairness of laying on capitalism or the free development of individual wealth the blame which is really due to the arbitrary and violent manner in which rights over land have been acquired and exercised, and to the failure of the state to fulfil those functions which under a system of unlimited private ownership are necessary to maintain the conditions of a free life.[45]

2

Green's concept of the proletariat is not strictly speaking of a class defined solely by the wealth or property of its members. What, then, is the distinguishing element of this class? What common characteristic of its individual members renders them a class? Green's answer reveals much about his theory of property and his social and political thought as a whole.

Green believes that a certain level of economic existence is required to enable man to conceive the action in himself of a spiritual principle, to be aware therefore of the possibility of a good consisting in something other than the satisfaction of his animal appetites. 'Until life has been so organized as to afford some regular relief from the pressure of animal wants,' he writes, 'an interest in what Aristotle calls ["living well"], as distinct from [merely "living"], cannot emerge.' In a generally low standard of living, men will not engage 'in the pursuit of ends to which life is a means, as distinct from the pursuit of means of living.'[46]

But Green holds that society has reached a level of economic life high enough to allow such 'regular relief' for all its members. The market economy was not in itself responsible for the creation of a proletariat; 'there is nothing in the nature of the case to keep these labourers in the condition of living from hand to mouth.'[47] On the contrary, because of the constant generation of new wealth, the market economy is

44 PPO, sec. 230; emphasis added
45 Ibid.; cf. Speech to the Wellington Lodge of Odd Fellows, February 1868, cited by Nettleship, 'Memoir,' *Works*, III, p. cxii.
46 PE, sec. 240. Cf. secs 241, 243, 248; and *Spencer & Lewes*, sec. 2.
47 PPO, sec. 227

best suited to their enrichment. Nevertheless, he acknowledges that in fact the members of the proletariat 'are owners of nothing beyond what is necessary from day to day for the support of life, and may at any time lose even that.'[48] He has noticed 'the poor person whose waking hours are spent in the struggle to keep his family respectable.'[49] Occupied primarily by the effort simply to survive, the proletarian has little chance of becoming conscious of a possible self and of his true good as consisting in its realization.

Green must accordingly explain how an impoverished class, unable to conceive the true good, has arisen. His solution, we have seen, is to ascribe its existence to 'antecedent circumstances'; the propertyless condition of industrial workers is a direct result of the confiscation of their land through force and conquest. More than this, however, seems to be implied in Green's analysis. The members of the labouring class are 'debased,'[50] 'degraded,'[51] 'reckless,'[52] 'men whose ancestors, if not themselves, were trained in the habits of serfdom.'[53] They have what Green might have called the 'mentality of serfdom.'

I suggest that this 'mentality,' this common consciousness, is for Green the distinguishing characteristic of the members of the proletariat. Landless and oppressed for so long, they are unable to perceive the value of property as a means of self-satisfaction and self-expression. Appropriation is for him a function of man's spiritual nature; the acquisition of permanent possessions implies that man is other and more than a merely sentient organism. In a primitive condition of society, then, in which the bare necessities of life are with difficulty obtained by anyone, a general rise in the level of economic existence is necessary before the idea of man's moral capacity may be conceived. But since in modern society, according to Green, property may be acquired by all, ownership of property is a kind of barometer of one's moral development, and the propertylessness of the proletariat is accordingly evidence of the retarded development of the members of this class.

In Green's estimation, therefore, the consciousness of the working class is not an outgrowth of their poverty; rather their poverty is the product of their consciousness. The problem of the proletariat is thus a problem, not of economics, but of consciousness. Proletarians neither own nor seek[54] property because they are not

48   PPO, sec. 226
49   PE, sec. 248
50   Speech to the Wellington Lodge of Odd Fellows, Feb. 1868, 'Memoir,' Works, III, p. cxii
51   'Liberal Legislation,' Works, III, p. 376
52   Speech to the Wellington Lodge of Odd Fellows, Feb. 1868, 'Memoir,' Works, III, p. cxii; and PPO, sec. 227. The proletariat is 'reckless' because its members do not have an adequate consciousness of self and hence are not sufficiently motivated to render their habitual obedience to the political authority.
53   PPO, sec. 229
54   PPO, sec. 230

wholly conscious of themselves as other than their physical wants; they live little
more than an animal existence because they do not see that they are reproductions
of the eternal self; they are not, we may say, truly self-conscious.

This position is reflected in Green's consideration of the working and living conditions of the labouring class. Many of the difficulties of its members are in his view
due not to outside causes but to their own inability to order their lives. Discussing,
for example, the need for legislation to assist the proletariat, he writes:

Left to itself, or to the operation of casual benevolence, a degraded population perpetuates
and increases itself ... Given a certain standard of moral and material well-being, people may
be *trusted* not to sell their labour, or the labour of their children, on terms which would allow
that standard to be maintained. But with large masses of our population, until the laws we
have been considering took effect, there was no such standard. There was nothing on their
part, in the way either of self-respect or established demand for comforts, to prevent them
from working and living, or from putting their children to work and live, in a way in which no
one who is to be a healthy and free citizen can work and live.[55]

In another context, he comments:

The individual's right to live is but the other side of the right which society has in his living.
The individual can no more voluntarily rid himself of it than he can of the social capacity, the
human nature, on which it is founded. Thus, however *ready* men may be for high wages to
work in a dangerous pit, a wrong is held to be done if they are killed in it. If provisions which
might have made it safe have been neglected, someone is held responsible. If nothing could
make it safe, the working of the pit would not be allowed. The reason for not more generally
applying the power of the state to prevent *voluntary* noxious employments, is not that there is
no wrong in the death of the individual through the incidents of an employment which he has
voluntarily undertaken, but that the wrong is more effectually prevented by training and
trusting individuals to protect themselves than by the state protecting them.[56]

Finally, we may note the following:

It is evident that in the body of school and factory legislation which I have noticed we have a
great system of interference with freedom of contract. The hirer of labour is prevented from
hiring it on terms to which the person of whom he hires it could for the most part have been
readily brought to agree. If children and young persons and women were not ready in many
cases, either from their own wish, or under the influence of parents and husbands, to accept

55 'Liberal Legislation,' *Works*, III, p. 376; emphasis added
56 PPO, sec. 159; emphasis added

employment of the kind which the law prohibits, there would have been no occasion for the prohibition.[57]

In all these cases the onus is clearly and consistently held to rest with the propertyless themselves: 'noxious employments' are 'voluntarily undertaken'; women and children 'accept' undesirable occupations 'either from their own wish, or under the influence of parents and husbands'; and, in a case not cited above, tenant-farmers have entered into contracts contrary to their own interests because they 'have either not been intelligent enough, or not independent enough.'[58] Furthermore, just as the members of the proletariat are themselves responsible for their economic predicament, in the sense that their failure to rectify it is a result of the underdeveloped state of their consciousness, so must they better themselves through their own effort:

There is nothing in the fact that their labour is hired in great masses by great capitalists to prevent them from being on a small scale capitalists themselves. In their position they have not indeed the same stimulus to saving, or the same constant opening for the investment of savings, as a man who is [self-employed]; but their combination in work gives them every opportunity, if they have the needful education and *self-discipline*, for forming societies for the investment of savings. In fact, as we know, in the well-paid industries of England *the better sort of labourers* do become capitalists, to the extent often of owning their houses and a good deal of furniture, of having an interest in stores, and of belonging to benefit-societies, through which they make provision for the future.[59]

This view also explains Green's somewhat unexpected attitude towards charitable institutions. Considering his rejection of selfishness as immoral and his belief in a

57 'Liberal Legislation,' *Works*, III, pp. 369-70
58 Ibid., p. 380; cf. pp. 379-82.
59 PPO, sec. 227; emphasis added. Cf. Speech to the Wellington Lodge of Odd Fellows, Feb. 1868, 'Memoir,' *Works*, III, p. cxii: 'the workmen, who can only secure themselves as I believe, by such a system of protection as is implied in the better sort of trades-union.' It is not entirely clear what Green intended by 'the better sort of trades-union.' He may have simply meant benefit societies; Melvin Richter cites evidence to indicate that he was against militant activity by labour. *The Politics of Conscience: T.H. Green and his Age* (London: Weidenfeld and Nicolson, 1964), pp. 328-9. Although his evidence is by no means definitive, this view is certainly consistent with the general tenor of Green's thought. In any event, support of moderate trade union activity cannot be said to have been a revolutionary position by any means. Indeed in the early 1870s, 'trade unions were given what amounted to their modern legal status, that is they were henceforth accepted as permanent and not in themselves noxious parts of the industrial scene.' E.J. Hobsbawm, *Industry and Empire* (Harmondsworth: Penguin Books, 1969), p. 125.
Green's suggestion that a labourer who has acquired a house or furniture has acquired *capital* is obviously mistaken and shows his failure to grasp economic concepts.

common good, one might have expected him to favour institutions through whose assistance the impoverished might very well become valuable contributing members of society. His opposition to philanthropy, however, is clear in his educational writings, where he suggests that such monies would be better spent on education even though the main beneficiary in that case would be the middle class.[60] Similarly, he includes the Poor Law – 'which takes away the occasion for the exercise of parental forethought, filial reverence, and neighbourly kindness' – in the category of laws 'which *check* the development of the moral disposition' rather than promote it.[61]

The view that the economic improvement of the labouring class must be *self-attained* follows directly from Green's contention that self-determination is a precondition of the realization of the true good. Charity or the benefits secured by the Poor Law 'check' the moralization of man because they inhibit the possibility of his freely and independently determining his life for himself. Similarly, the provision of property to the individual by society is incompatible with this possibility. In the final analysis, therefore, it is the inability of the proletarian to better himself even with the free play afforded by the market economy to his powers of appropriation that renders him a proletarian.

Thus, in the modern state, according to Green, economic conditions do not determine consciousness; consciousness determines economic conditions. The proletarian is not, in Green's sense, self-conscious; he cannot adequately conceive his possible, his real, self. He is thus unable to direct his will, his effort to achieve self-satisfaction, to the attainment of his true good; his will, Green would say, is not in conformity with his reason. In so far, then, as ownership of property is a measure of one's ability to conceive the true good and of one's success in realizing that good – of the extent, in other words, to which one's will is directed by reason – the individual who is propertyless, the proletarian, may truly be said to be relatively less rational than the property-owner.

On the other hand the property-owner has demonstrated by his appropriation that he is conscious of himself as more than an animal organism, that he is at least capable of conceiving his true good, although he may not yet have conceived it fully. Relative to the proletarian, he is more rational and therefore closer to the realization of his capacities.

Accordingly, the solution of the problem of the labouring class, the elimination, that is, of 'an impoverished and reckless proletariate,' is only to be achieved, in Green's view, through a fundamental transformation of the consciousness of its

60 *Schools Inquiry Commission* (London: George E. Eyre and William Spottiswoode, for Her Majesty's Stationery Office, 1868-9), VIII, pp. 218, 224, 232-3; and XV, p. 696; and 'Lecture on the Work to be Done by the New Oxford High School for Boys,' *Works*, III, p. 456
61 PPO, sec. 17; emphasis added. See also sec. 229.

members. The transition from propertyless to property-owning involves, as we have seen, much more than the mere act of acquisition. The legislative reform he deemed necessary to facilitate this transformation will be considered in the next chapter.

3

Bearing directly on Green's theory of social classes is legislation concerning property in land. The existence of a proletariat, we have seen, is attributed by Green to 'influences of feudalism and landlordism,' to 'the arbitrary and violent manner in which rights over land have been acquired and exercised.'[62] He sees this not as an argument against unlimited private ownership in land, but as a sign that 'rights have been allowed to landlords, incompatible with the true principle on which rights of property rest.'[63] Moreover, the nature of land made this situation a special one:

the question in regard to land stands on a different footing from that in regard to wealth generally, owing to the fact that land is a particular commodity limited in extent, from which alone can be derived the materials necessary to any industry whatever, on which men must find house-room if they are to find it at all, and over which they must pass in communicating with each other, however much water or even air may be used for that purpose. These are indeed not reasons for preventing private property in land or even free bequest of land, but they necessitate a *special control* over the exercise of rights of property in land.[64]

The problem, according to Green, is that 'though a growing reduction in the number of landlords is not necessarily a social evil ... that full development of [the land's] resources, which individual ownership would naturally favour has been interfered with by laws and customs which, in securing estates to certain families, have taken away the interest, and tied the hands, of the nominal owner – the tenant for life – in making the most of his property.'[65] Thus, he argues, 'since most of us grew up there has been no exchangeable commodity in England except land – no doubt a large exception – of which the exchange has not been perfectly free.'[66] 'The only effectual reform of the land laws,' accordingly, 'is to put a stop to those settlements or bequests by which at present a landlord may prevent his successor from either converting any part of his land into money or from dividing it among his children.'[67]

62 PPO, sec. 230
63 PPO, sec. 229
64 PPO, sec. 231; emphasis added. Cf. 'Liberal Legislation,' *Works*, III, p. 377.
65 PPO, sec. 229; cf. sec. 210.
66 'Liberal Legislation,' *Works*, III, p. 368
67 Ibid., p. 366

At the present the greater part of the land of England is held under settlements which prevent the nominal owner from either dividing his land among his children or from selling any part of it for their benefit. It is so settled that all of it necessarily goes to the owner's eldest son ... The evil effects of this system are twofold. In the first place it almost entirely prevents the sale of agricultural land in small quantities, and thus hinders the formation of that mainstay of social order and contentment, a class of small proprietors. Secondly it keeps large quantities of land in the hands of men who are too much burdened by debts or family charges to improve it. The landlord in such cases has not the money to improve, the tenant has not the security which would justify him in improving. Thus a great part of the land of England is left in a state in which, according to such eminent and impartial authorities as lord Derby and lord Leicester, it does not yield half of what it might.[68]

Green proposes, therefore, 'that legal sanction should be withheld for the future from settlements which thus interfere with the distribution and improvement of land'[69]; freedom of bequest, in other words, should be limited so far as it tends to obstruct the free play of the powers of individual appropriation. 'Such a change' he suggests 'would render English land on the whole a much more marketable commodity than it is at present.'[70] He argues, further, on behalf of 'such tenant-right as would secure to the out-going tenant the full value of unexhausted improvements,'[71] a measure that in his view would increase the productivity of the land by providing for the 'due application of capital to the soil.'[72] We may note, additionally, Green's contention that the '"unearned increment" in the value of the soil' should not be 'appropriated by the state,' because such a system 'could scarcely be established without lessening the stimulus to the individual to make the most of the land, and thus ultimately lessening its serviceableness to society.'[73] Thus, despite the language in which they are couched, Green's recommendations for 'a special control over the exercise of rights of property in land,' far from limiting 'individual liberty,' are clearly designed to hasten the development of capitalist methods of production in the cultivation and general use of the land.

The picture Green draws of the consequences of 'unrestricted landlordism'[74] is not especially flattering. He implies a somewhat vaguely defined class of 'land-lords'[75] whose members are characterized by extreme selfishness and lack of social

68 Ibid., p. 378
69 Ibid., pp. 378-9
70 Ibid., p. 379
71 Ibid., p. 381
72 Ibid., p. 380
73 PPO, sec. 232
74 PPO, sec. 230
75 PPO, sec. 229

conscience, who seek a particular rather than a general good. Evidently the consciousness of this class, like that of the proletariat, is inconsistent with the realization of the true good. In so far as he has acquired property, the landlord is more rational than the proletarian; however, in so far as his will is directed to a merely personal good he may be said to be less rational than the individual striving to actualize the true good. Indeed, Green asserts, the motive of this proposed legislation is 'the same old cause of social good against class interests, for which, under altered names, liberals are fighting now as they were fifty years ago.'[76]

4

From Green's theory of property emerges a thoroughgoing justification of the capitalist market economy. Though he criticizes many of the assumptions of the liberal tradition – property as a natural, i.e. personal, right; the good as consisting in the accumulation of pleasures; man as essentially a consumer of utilities – Green shares the liberals' unshakeable belief in the moral value and legitimacy of capitalism. Indeed, his Idealism, rather than providing a foundation for the critical evaluation of his society, serves, in effect, to justify its laws and institutions.

Green's tendency to support the status quo was shown also in his opposition to political resistance, which betrayed an overriding concern for political stability, for the maintenance of existing governments. This analysis may be extended to the whole of his political theory. It is a justification of nineteenth-century English society. The modern state in this view is the highest form of human society: its laws are the work of reason; the rights it recognizes allow man to realize his true good; and the 'general will,' upon which the whole edifice rests, becomes in Green's hand a perversion of Rousseau's idea – from a principle of incisive social criticism it is transformed into an instrument of legitimization.

Green's theory of property implies a similar acceptance of the rationality of his society's economic system, i.e. the capitalist market economy. All the essential elements of that system – personal independence (self-determination), private property in one's person and possessions, the right of unlimited individual acquisition – are duly considered and defended, with little or no thought to their possible incompatibility with his concept of the ultimate good. Perhaps he never abandoned his early notion of the permanence and invariability of economic laws. 'The recognition of the laws of political economy' he wrote in 1858 'is in itself an admission that men have no control over the results of their own combined energies, which operate in a system as independent of human will as that which regulates the motion of the heavenly bodies.'[77]

76 'Liberal Legislation,' Works, III, p. 367
77 'The Force of Circumstances,' Works, III, p. 9

Capitalism therefore appears to play a much more profound role in Green's thought than has hitherto been noted. Green sees in the capitalist economic system a perfect paradigm for his theory of self-realization: the free market system represents in the economic sphere what the state does in the political sphere and the true good in the ethical sphere.[78] Just as the individual, in striving to perfect himself or in rendering habitual obedience to the state, is for Green contributing to the realization of a good that is both personal and social, so does he, in freely exercising his powers of personal appropriation, contribute to the economic well-being of society as a whole. Similarly, just as both the true good and the state mediate between private and common interests, merging them in a sense, so does the market mediate between particular and general interests. Capitalism is for Green the truly rational economic system.

Moreover, the capitalist class represents to Green a state of mind: on one hand, unlike the proletariat, a consciousness of self as transcending one's animal existence and thus requiring permanent and secure possessions to achieve true self-satisfaction; on the other hand, unlike the landlord class, a consciousness of personal good as consisting in the good of all members of society. The individual capitalist may not have an adequate conception of his possible self or of his true good. However, he personifies the realizer and developer of his capacities. His ownership of property and his full participation in the market constitute evidence of the activity in him of the spiritual principle and indeed show that its presence is much stronger in him than in the proletarian or landlord.

The capitalist class is for Green the universal class – truly representative of the interests of all persons and in possibility including all persons – because in fulfilling its economic function it contributes to the realization of the ultimate good. Again, the individual capitalist may be actuated by merely selfish passions and to that extent contribute less to the common good than he might. Nevertheless, in so far as he carries out his economic function, in so far as he conforms to the economic laws of the market, his will conforms to the dictates of reason, and he may be said to be rational. Even the trader involved in 'objectionable transactions,' who profits by the cheapness of goods which 'arises from the presence of labourers who have no alternative but to work for "starvation wages"' Green maintains 'is profiting by what is at the same time a contribution to social well-being.'[79]

Finally, Green's ultimate solution of the problem of the proletariat is a classless (or, what amounts to the same thing, a one-class) society. 'The work of the reformer progresses' he writes 'as the social force is brought to bear more and more fully on classes and individuals, merging distinctions of privilege and position in one social

---

78 And, Green would add, Christianity in the religious sphere.
79 PPO, sec. 224. Cf. secs 217, 229.

organism.'[80] Legislation designed to erode the power of the feudal aristocracy – the power that created a proletariat – both economically and, we shall see, politically by extending the franchise, would more fully integrate landlords into the market economy. As well, reform legislation would transform members of the labouring class into full-fledged capitalists. By these means Green hoped that a truly 'just' society would be established.[81]

Green freely admits that there must be economic inequality, that indeed such inequality is a prerequisite for the realization by individuals of their unique capacities. But his theory of social classes – defined not in the classical liberal manner by the source of their wealth (land, capital, or only one's own labour), but by the shared consciousness of their members – enabled him to contend that society could be classless, in the sense that all of its members share a common consciousness, a common purpose, and an equal possibility of perfecting themselves. What Green did not perceive is the fundamental incompatibility between his theory of the true good and capitalist market society, between man as self-realizer and market man. This contradiction, we shall see, was the fatal flaw in his analysis.

80 'An Estimate of the Value and Influence of Works of Fiction in Modern Times,' *Works*, III, p. 41
81 ' "The just" = that complex of social conditions which for each individual is necessary to enable him to realize his capacity of contributing to social good.' PPO, sec. 186, n. 1

6

The theory of human nature

The interpretation of Green's theory of social classes presented in the last chapter is confirmed by his program for legislative reform. His proposals for land legislation, through which he hoped to remove what he conceived to be the primary cause for the existence of a proletariat, the feudal aristocracy, have already been discussed. In addition, however, Green saw the need to deal directly with the effects of 'unrestricted landlordism.' His recommendations for legislation, therefore, had a twofold purpose: first, to alleviate the intolerable physical hardships of the labouring class; and, second, to diminish the mental degradation of the proletariat, moralize its members, and thereby make them responsible, contributing citizens of market society.

This dual theme of physical and moral improvement may be traced throughout Green's discussion of social reform. He saw it as the proper aim of legislation in such areas as the health, housing, and workplaces of the labouring class[1]: guaranteeing to the proletarian certain concrete benefits that the underdeveloped state of his consciousness prevents him from securing for himself, and creating an environment more conducive to moral development by eliminating those elements of his existence which might cause him to sink even further into a state of hopeless degradation.

The same goal lay before his reform proposals in the two chief areas of his concern, temperance legislation and reform of the educational system, to which most of his effort on behalf of reform, both practical and theoretical, was devoted. The ameliorative possibilities of these reforms on the physical and economic situation of the labouring class may be self-evident, but their relation to Green's theory of social classes and consciousness should be more closely examined.

---

1 See, for example, PPO, secs 210, 230; 'Liberal Legislation,' *Works*, III, pp. 365-6, 369-70, 373-4; and PE, sec. 332.

Green joined the United Kingdom Alliance in 1872 and later became vice-president of the organization. In 1875 he established a coffee tavern and was made treasurer of the Oxford Diocesan Branch of the Church of England Temperance Society. He became president of the Oxford Band of Hope Temperance Union in 1876.[2]

Although Green recognizes drunkenness to be an affliction not confined to the labouring class – his own brother was an alcoholic[3] – Green seems to identify it very closely with the proletariat. He sees it as a cause of the lowering of moral standards and hence of economic well-being. 'Drunkenness in the head of a family' he contends 'means, as a rule, the impoverishment and degradation of all members of the family.'[4] The poor, whose consciousness is already underdeveloped, are particularly susceptible to alcoholism. Speaking of the proletariat, he writes: 'Their health, housing and schooling were unprovided for. They were left to be freely victimized by deleterious employments, foul air, and *consequent* craving for deleterious drinks.'[5]

A drunken population naturally perpetuates and increases itself. Many families, it is true, keep emerging from *the conditions which render them specially liable* to the evil habit, but on the other hand, descent through drunkenness from respectability to squalor is constantly going on ... Better education, better housing, more healthy rules of labour, no doubt lessen the temptation to drink for those who have the benefit of these advantages, but meanwhile drunkenness is constantly recruiting the ranks of those who *cannot* be really educated, who *will not* be better housed, who *make* their employments dangerous and unhealthy. An effectual liquor law in short is the necessary complement of our factory acts, our education acts, our public health acts.[6]

Indeed, the symptoms of alcoholism seem to epitomize for Green the proletarian condition: lack of independence, no sense of personal or family responsibility, lack of true self-consciousness, and as a result enslavement by one's animal appetites, by the lower aspects of human nature. While the solution therefore must 'involve a large interference with the liberty of the individual to do as he likes in the matter of buying and selling alcohol,'[7] there is no alternative if the impoverished are to be rescued from their predicament and the reforms already enacted to have any lasting effect. 'There is no right to freedom in the purchase and sale of a particular commodity, if the general result of allowing such freedom is to detract from freedom in

2 R.L. Nettleship, 'Memoir,' *Works*, III, p. cxv
3 Ibid., p. cxvii.
4 'Liberal Legislation,' *Works*, III, p. 384
5 PPO, sec. 230; emphasis added. Cf. 'Memoir,' *Works*, III, pp. cxvii-cxviii.
6 'Liberal Legislation,' *Works*, III, p. 385; emphasis added
7 Ibid., p. 383

the higher sense, from the general power of men to make the best of themselves.'[8] In fact, Green maintains, temperance legislation, 'along with the effectual liberation of the soil, is the next great conquest which our democracy, on behalf of its own true freedom, has to make.'[9]

Green's early and continuing interest in the reform of the school system appears to stem from his service as an assistant commissioner to the Schools Inquiry Commission in 1865-6.[10] He was elected to the Oxford School Board in 1874[11] and was instrumental in the establishment of the Oxford High School for Boys.[12] In addition, he delivered a number of lectures on the subject of educational reform.[13]

The true aim of education in Green's view is the creation of 'a socially united people,'[14] which is to be accomplished on two levels. First, since classes are essentially the product of diverse mentalities, class conflict is the result of a lack of understanding between classes. In one of his early essays, he writes:

The most wounding social wrongs more often arise from ignorance than from malice, from acquiescence in the opinion of a class rather than from deliberate selfishness. The master cannot enter into the feelings of the servant, nor the servant into those of his master. The master cannot understand how any good quality can lead one to 'forget his station'; to the servant the spirit of management in the master seems mere 'driving.' This is only a sample of what is going on all society over. The relation between the higher and lower classes becomes irritating, and therefore injurious, not from any conscious unfairness on either side, but simply from the want of a common understanding; while at the same time every class suffers within its own limits from the prevalence of habits and ideas under the authority of class-

8 Ibid.; cf. PE, sec. 265.
9 'Liberal Legislation,' *Works*, III, p. 386
10 · 'Memoir,' *Works*, III, pp. xlv-lviii. See Green's reports in *Schools Inquiry Commission*, (London: George E. Eyre and William Spottiswoode, for Her Majesty's Stationery Office, 1868-9), VIII (General Report on the Schools in the Counties of Stafford and Warwick, and Special Report on King Edward VI Free School, Birmingham), XII (Reports on the Counties of Buckingham and Northampton), XV (Reports on the Counties of Stafford and Warwick), and XVI (Report on the County of Leicester).
11 'Memoir,' *Works*, III, pp. cxiv-cxv
12 Ibid., p. cxix. See also Benjamin Jowett, *Sermons Biographical and Miscellaneous*, ed. by W.H. Fremantle (London: John Murray, 1899), p. 221.
13 Speech on the program of the National Education League, at Oxford, 27 Jan. 1870, cited by Nettleship, 'Memoir,' *Works*, III, pp. cxiii-cxiv; 'The Grading of Secondary Schools' (1870), *Works*, III; Two Lectures on 'The Elementary School System of England' (1878), *Works*, III; and 'The Work to be Done by the New Oxford High School for Boys' (1882), *Works*, III. See also Green's Testimony, 30 Oct. 1877, *University of Oxford Commission, Part I: Minutes of Evidence Taken by the Commissioners Together with an Appendix and Index* (London: George Edward Eyre and William Spottiswoode, for Her Majesty's Stationery Office, 1881), pp. 200-5.
14 'The Work to be Done by the New Oxford High School for Boys,' *Works*, III, p. 456; cf. p. 460.

convention, which could not long maintain themselves if once placed in the light of general opinion.[15]

Social differences and class conflict, far from being eliminated by the educational system, were in Green's opinion being intensified and aggravated by it. 'The lines of education at present' he argued 'do not intersect the social strata, but are parallel with them. A boy is sent to the school which the means of his parents or their social expectations determine, and from it he very rarely emerges, except into another of the same sort, till his education is supposed to be finished.'[16] His reports to the Schools Inquiry Commission overflow with examples of the separation of classes and of the unwillingness of parents to have their children mix with those of 'inferior' classes.[17] The removal of class divisions in society at large therefore presupposes their prior elimination within the school system itself:

Common education is the true social leveller. Men and women who have been at school together, or who have been at schools of the same sort, will always understand each other, will always be at their ease together, will be free from social jealousies and animosities however different their circumstances in life may be. In every nation, perhaps, there must be a certain separation between those who live solely by the labour of their heads or by the profits of capital, between members of the learned professions and those engaged constantly in buying and selling, between those who are earning their money and those who are living on the income of large accumulated capital; but in England these separations have been fixed and deepened by the fact that there has been no fusion of class with class in school or at the universities.[18]

At a more profound level, education serves as a social leveller by equipping the children of the poor with those tools by means of which they may moralize them-

15 'An Estimate of the Value and Influence of Works of Fiction in Modern Times,' *Works*, III, p. 42; cf. 'The Work to be Done by the New Oxford High School for Boys,' *Works*, III, p. 458.
16 'The Grading of Secondary Schools,' *Works*, III, p. 390; cf. pp. 403, 412.
17 *Schools Inquiry Commission*, VIII, pp. 131, 133, 141, 159, 161-2, 190, 222; XII, pp. 180, 325; XV, pp. 365, 385, 395, 440, 714, 747; XVI, p. 28. Cf. 'The Work to be Done by the New Oxford High School for Boys,' *Works*, III, p. 462.
   Referring to his experiences as an assistant commissioner, Green wrote: 'I was then looking forward, in common with many of those with whom I was associated at Oxford, to a reconstitution, at no very distant time, of the middle and higher education of England, and, as I need not be ashamed to add, if not to a reconstitution of society through that of education, yet at least to a considerable change in its tone and to the removal of many of its barriers.' 'The Grading of Secondary Schools,' *Works*, III, p. 387
18 'The Work to be Done by the New Oxford High School for Boys,' *Works*, III, pp. 457-8; cf. pp. 460, 475-6. See also, *Schools Inquiry Commission*, XV, pp. 388, 420; XVI, p. 21.

selves and thereby escape the debasement of their parents. Thus, Green asserts, 'the neglect of [education] does tend to prevent the growth of the capacity for beneficially exercising rights on the part of those whose education is neglected.'[19] 'Without a command of certain elementary arts and knowledge, the individual in modern society is as effectually crippled as by the loss of a limb or a broken constitution. He is not free to develop his capacities.'[20] As a result, education is a matter of concern to all members of society:

to everyone who cares for the future of his country, everyone whose patriotism is of a higher order than that which finds expression in hooting the Russian czar, the question, with what sort of mental equipment the children of the next generation are to go into the world, must be of supreme interest. Under God, it is to good books and a knowledge of the laws of nature that we must chiefly trust to make them, when they become their own masters, healthy and wise and virtuous.[21]

The problem is that private enterprise, working through the laws of supply and demand, cannot, in Green's opinion, meet the needs of an adequate educational system.[22] Indeed, he maintains, 'all orders of society above the lowest can be trusted to find for themselves the education which the maintenance of their social position requires'[23]; but '"it is precisely those who need education most that are least capable of demanding it, desiring it, or even conceiving of it."'[24] At the same time, Green insists, modern methods of industrial production make it practically impossible for parents, especially those of the labouring class, to educate their own children:

In an ideal society, perhaps, the education of all families might safely be left under the control, in each case, of the parents. In the actual state of English society, however, no one pretends that it can be so left, and it is doubtful whether under the modern system of labour in great masses, which draws all who have to work for their living more and more away from their homes, the fate of the children can ever with safety be left solely in the hands of the parents.[25]

For these reasons, then, as well as to remove its division along class lines, the educational system must be brought under social control. 'With a view to securing

19 PPO, sec. 209
20 'Liberal Legislation,' Works, III, pp. 373-4
21 'The Elementary School System of England: II.' Works, III, p. 454
22 Schools Inquiry Commission, VIII, pp. 111, 194-5, 207
23 'The Grading of Secondary Schools,' Works, III, p. 389
24 Quoted by Green (no reference given), 'The Elementary School System of England: I,' Works, III, p. 428. Cf. below, p. 137, at note 33.
25 Ibid., pp. 431-2.

such freedom among its members it is as certainly within the province of the state to prevent children from growing up in that kind of ignorance which practically excludes them from a free career in life, as it is within its province to require the sort of building and drainage necessary for public health.'[26]

Green considered political reform as well. Although he wrote very little on the subject, such reform received his full support. He drew a direct relation between the First and Second Reform Acts and the social legislation of the nineteenth century.[27] He spoke of the need for the greater democratization of parliament, both through a further extension of the franchise[28] and by reducing the cost of elections. 'As long as we have a parliament,' Green stated in early 1882, 'which is in fact a sort of club of rich men, we shall not have a parliament which has the interest of the struggling and suffering classes of society at heart.'[29]

The dual theme of physical and moral improvement of the poor also underlies Green's defence of political reform. The purpose of such reform is not only to make possible the enactment of measures to improve the circumstances of the proletariat but further to awaken in man, through his participation in the political process, an interest in the common good:

That active interest in the service of the state, which makes patriotism in the better sense, can hardly arise while the individual's relation to the state is that of a passive recipient of protection in the exercise of his rights of person and property. While this is the case, he will give the state no thanks for the protection which he will come to take as a matter of course, and will only be conscious of it when it descends upon him with some unusual demand for service or payment, and then he will be conscious of it in the way of resentment. If he is to have a higher feeling of political duty, he must take part in the work of the state. He must have a share, direct or indirect, by himself acting as a member or by voting for the members of supreme or provincial assemblies, in making and maintaining the laws which he obeys. Only thus will he learn to regard the work of the state as a whole, and to transfer to the whole the interest which otherwise his particular experience would lead him to feel only in that part of its work that goes to the maintenance of his own and his neighbour's rights.[30]

26 'Liberal Legislation,' *Works*, III, p. 374. Cf. 'The Elementary School System of England: I,' *Works*, III, p. 432; 'The Elementary School System of England: II,' *Works*, III, pp. 454-5; and PPO, sec. 209.

27 'Liberal Legislation,' *Works*, III, pp. 368-9; 'The Elementary School System of England: I,' *Works*, III, pp. 415, 418. See also PPO, sec. 229, where Green argues that property rights have been granted to the feudal aristocracy which are inconsistent with the idea of property, 'from government having been chiefly in the hands of appropriators of the soil.'

28 'The Elementary School System of England: I,' *Works*, III, p. 418

29 Speech to the North Ward Liberal Association, 10 Jan. 1882, cited by Nettleship, 'Memoir,' *Works*, III, p. cxix

30 PPO, sec. 122

Political participation is for Green a process of moralization, through which man becomes truly conscious of himself and of his true good as consisting in the common good. It follows that such participation is an instrument – indeed, a precondition – of the moral edification of the masses. Speaking of the Reform Act of 1867, Green commented:

We who were reformers from the beginning, always said that the enfranchisement of the people was an end in itself. We said, and we were much derided for saying so, that citizenship *only* makes the moral man; that citizenship *only* gives that self-respect, which is the true basis of respect for others, and without which there is no lasting social order or real morality. If we were asked what result we looked for from the enfranchisement of the people, we said, that is not the present question; untie the man's legs, and then it will be time to speculate how he will walk.[31]

The aim of Green's program of reform is 'not indeed directly to promote moral goodness, for that, from the very nature of moral goodness, it cannot do, but to maintain the conditions without which a free exercise of the human faculties is impossible.'[32] Because the labourer is unable adequately to order his life, society must do all it can to create the conditions necessary for his moralization. 'No one can convey a good character to another,' Green asserts. 'Every one must make his character for himself. All that one man can do to make another better is to remove obstacles and supply conditions favourable to the formation of good character.'[33] More than that society cannot do – must not do – and still hope to bring about that transformation of the consciousness of the proletarian that will make him a realizer of his capacities and an asset to society as a whole. Referring to the social legislation of his century, he remarks:

Act after act was passed preventing master and workman, parent and child, house-builder and householder, from doing as they pleased, with the result of a great addition to the real freedom of society. The spirit of self-reliance and independence was not weakened by those

31 Speech to the Wellington Lodge of Odd Fellows, Feb. 1868, cited by Nettleship, 'Memoir,' *Works*, III, p. cxii. It should be noted that Green never, as far as I am aware, declared himself in favour of universal manhood suffrage, although the logic of his argument would appear to imply such support. Similarly, he gave no opinion on the subject of the enfranchisement of women. His only reference to women's rights is extremely vague and makes no mention of political rights. See PE, sec. 267. Green, it should be recalled, died in 1882, two years before the passage of the Third Reform Bill.
32 'Liberal Legislation,' *Works*, III, p. 374; cf. PPO, sec. 18.
33 PE, sec. 332, Cf. PPO, secs 11, 209; and Speech to the North Ward Liberal Association, 10 Jan. 1882, 'Memoir,' *Works*, III, p. cxx.

acts. Rather it received a new development. The dead weight of ignorance and unhealthy surroundings, with which it would otherwise have had to struggle, being partially removed by law, it was more free to exert itself for higher objects.[34]

2

At this point Green is compelled to come to terms with what appears at first to be an inconsistency in his argument: his defence of social reform seems founded on a rejection of one of the fundamental freedoms of the market system, the freedom of contract. Green himself readily admits that by 'limit[ing] a man's power of doing what he will with what he considers his own,'[35] the reforms of nineteenth-century England constituted 'a great system of interference with freedom of contract.'[36] The problem in his view is that, as a result of the underdeveloped moral state of the proletariat, the strict enforcement of freedom of contract had in the past led to injustices being committed. 'To uphold the sanctity of contracts' he writes, with reference to the Irish farmers, 'is doubtless a prime business of government, but it is no less its business to provide against contracts being made which, from the help-lessness of one of the parties to them, instead of being a security for freedom, become an instrument of disguised oppression.'[37] Green was of course hardly an opponent of the free market economy. How then does he reconcile the two positions? What justification does he provide for his recommendations for reform?

At this stage Green introduces his third concept of freedom:

We shall probably all agree that freedom, rightly understood, is the greatest of blessings; that its attainment is the true end of all our effort as citizens. But when we thus speak of freedom, we should consider carefully what we mean by it. We do not mean merely freedom from restraint or compulsion. We do not mean merely freedom to do as we like irrespectively of what it is that we like. We do not mean a freedom that can be enjoyed by one man or one set of men at the cost of a loss of freedom to others. When we speak of freedom as something to be so highly prized, we mean a positive power or capacity of doing or enjoying something worth doing or enjoying, and that, too, something that we do or enjoy in common with others. We mean by it a power which each man exercises through the help or security given him by his fellow-men, and which he in turn helps to secure for them.[38]

34 'Liberal Legislation,' *Works*, III, pp. 385-6
35 Ibid., p. 366
36 Ibid., p. 369; cf. PPO, sec. 210.
37 'Liberal Legislation,' *Works*, III, p. 382
38 Ibid., pp. 370-1. Commenting on this passage, Kenneth R. Hoover writes: 'The significant element here is the introduction of the term *power* into the definition of the term *freedom*. An individual without the tools to make his way in the world is not free. The power of the state

He continues:

> If I have given a true account of that freedom which forms the goal of social effort, we shall see that freedom of contract, freedom in all the forms of doing what one will with one's own, is valuable only as a means to an end. That end is what I call freedom in the positive sense: in other words, the liberation of the powers of all men equally for contributions to a common good. No one has a right to do what he will with his own in such a way as to contravene this end. It is only through the guarantee which society gives him that he has property at all, or, strictly speaking, any right to his possessions. This guarantee is founded on a sense of common interest. Every one has an interest in securing to every one else the free use and enjoyment and disposal of his possessions, as long as that freedom on the part of one does not interfere with a like freedom on the part of others, because such freedom contributes to that equal development of the faculties of all which is the highest good of all. This is the true and only justification of rights of property.[39]

Freedom of contract, 'freedom in all the forms of doing what one will with one's own,' is 'valuable' only as contributing to the actualization of 'that freedom which forms the goal of social effort.' The former 'freedom,' consisting in the free play of the powers of individual appropriation afforded by the market system, is predicated upon, and may in a sense be said to correspond to, Green's concept of 'moral freedom': the freedom of the will, of self-determination, which all persons possess merely by virtue of their humanity. On one hand it is because of his moral freedom, we have seen, that man requires 'the free use and enjoyment and disposal of his possessions' to realize his true good; on the other hand it is only in so far as all persons are morally free that the capitalist system may be deemed to be a just one, for the market economy assumes that all buyers and sellers are, at some minimal level, equally able to determine and order their own lives, to be independent – that they are able in other words 'to shift for themselves.'[40]

Even the proletarian is morally free. To be self-determining, however, is not necessarily to have an accurate or even a remotely accurate concept of self or of the good in which self-satisfaction is to be found. By virtue of his moral freedom, man is free to act for good or ill, free to seek his good in objects which are virtuous or vicious. What the proletarian lacks, therefore, is an adequate concept of self, true

must be deployed to liberate the individual's own resources for moral activity.' 'Liberalism and the Idealist Philosophy of Thomas Hill Green,' *Western Political Quarterly*, XXVI: No. 3 (Sept. 1973), p. 560. However, Hoover's contention that Green believed the state should provide the individual with 'the tools to make his way in the world' is clearly mistaken, as we shall see.

39 'Liberal Legislation,' *Works*, III, p. 372
40 Green's exact phrase is 'the freedom of every one to shift for himself.' PE, sec. 271. No acknowledgment is made to Locke.

self-consciousness, and this shortcoming, given the unrestricted freedom of contract, handicaps him in his dealings with unscrupulous individuals and makes it so much harder for him to overcome his degradation:

> It was the overworked women, the ill-housed and untaught families, for whose benefit [these laws] were intended. And the question is whether without these laws the suffering classes could have been delivered quickly or slowly from the condition they were in. Could the enlightened self-interest or benevolence of individuals, working under a system of unlimited freedom of contract, have ever brought them into a state compatible with the free development of the human faculties? No one considering the facts can have any doubt as to the answer to this question. Left to itself, or to the operation of casual benevolence, a degraded population perpetuates and increases itself ... If labour is to be had under conditions incompatible with the health or decent housing or education of the labourer, there will always be plenty of people to buy it under those conditions, careless of the burden in the shape of rates and taxes which they may be laying up for posterity. Either the standard of well-being on the part of the sellers of labour must prevent them from selling their labour under those conditions, or the law must prevent it. With a population such as ours was forty years ago, and still largely is, the law must prevent it and continue the prevention for some generations, before the sellers will be in a state to prevent it for themselves.[41]

Freedom 'in the positive sense,' therefore, is the basis both of the free play of the powers of individual appropriation and of such interference with that free play as is necessary to ensure that it does not become an impediment to self-realization on the part of some members of society, for this freedom constitutes 'the true end of all our efforts as citizens' and indeed of all human endeavour. To be sure, in proportion as all members of society are able to form an adequate conception of self and of the true good, in proportion, that is, as they become rational, their wills will tend to coincide – they will all tend to seek their self-satisfaction in the true good – and there will be no need to curtail the free exercise of their powers. On the contrary, such curtailment would then be an obstacle to the perfecting of men. However, in the prevailing conditions of English society, interference with the free market system was in Green's view both necessary and justifiable.

Freedom 'in the positive sense' corresponds quite clearly to Green's concept of 'real or higher freedom':

– It is 'a *positive* power or capacity of doing or enjoying,'[42] not 'merely freedom from restraint or compulsion.' It is the active and positive pursuit of good, the

---

41 'Liberal Legislation,' *Works*, III, p. 376-7
42 The definition of freedom cited in this paragraph is from ibid., pp. 370-1; all emphasis added.

freedom to do, to enjoy, to develop, as opposed to the freedom simply to be left alone.[43]

– It is the freedom to do or enjoy 'something *worth* doing or enjoying,' not 'merely freedom to do as we like irrespectively of what it is that we like.' In other words it is the pursuit of a good which is truly self-satisfying, self-determining in accordance with a true concept of self, as opposed to 'mere' self-determination or moral freedom.

– It is the freedom to do or enjoy 'something that we do or enjoy *in common with others*,' not 'a freedom that can be enjoyed by one man or one set of men at the cost of a loss of freedom to others.' Thus, it is the pursuit of a personal good that is at the same time a shared good, a good that is personally satisfying only in so far as it satisfies others as well, as opposed to a good that is exclusive and can only be achieved at the expense of others.

3

Green's theory of social classes, of the malleability and mutability of human consciousness, is founded on a concept of human nature as comprising two parts, two aspects. This dual nature was briefly alluded to in the consideration of the philosophical foundations of Green's thought, as well as in the discussion of his theory of self-realization. There it was pointed out that, according to his theory of knowledge, the process of man's coming to know his world, the cosmos of experience, is the process of an animal organism gradually becoming the vehicle of the divine consciousness; similarly, man's moral development, his growing awareness of his potentialities and of his true good, is the process of his transition from his actual to his possible self, from his limited animal existence to the full realization of his capacities. '"Our consciousness"' Green writes 'may mean either of two things; either a function of the animal organism, which is being made, gradually and with interruptions, a vehicle of the eternal consciousness, or that eternal consciousness itself, as making the animal organism its vehicle and subject to certain limitations in so doing.'[44]

It is as a part of nature, as a sentient being, in Green's view, that man has animal appetites. Limited by his physical existence, he is unable to transcend the limitations of the flesh, unable to see beyond his own personal, selfish ends, the satisfaction of his immediate desires for pleasure or the removal of pain. These desires, it is true,

43 Cf. PPO, sec. 25: 'Rights are what may be called the *negative* realization of [the power of the individual to make a common good his own]. That is, they realize it in the sense of providing for its free exercise, of securing the treatment of one man by another as equally free with himself, but they do not realize it *positively*, because their possession does not imply that in any active way the individual makes a common good his own.' Emphasis added

44 PE, sec. 67. Cf. *Hume I*, sec. 152; and 'Review of J. Caird,' *Works*, III, p. 145.

are more than *merely* animal desires since man, as human, and thus as partaking of the eternal mind, transforms them through their presence to his consciousness; indeed, it is only by virtue of this consciousness that he may truly be said to be selfish.[45] Nevertheless, having their origin in his animal nature, they are in a sense independent of man's spiritual being, though affected by it.

It is, however, as more than the product of natural events, as the vehicle of the eternal consciousness, that man has a spiritual nature and is able to transcend the limitations of his earthly, animal existence. He is, we have seen, eternal, self-conscious, and self-determining, and for this reason he cannot find true self-satisfaction in the gratification of his animal appetites, in pleasure or the means to the acquisition of further pleasure. Moreover, his good must be a common good, a good that is personally satisfying only in so far as it contributes to the well-being of his fellow men.

Green's concept of man, therefore, is of two fundamentally antagonistic aspects, or natures, coexisting within one being, one organism. On the one hand man is essentially a self-seeking, appetitive creature, who seeks his good in the accumulation of pleasures and thus in competition with and at the expense of others. On the other hand, opposed to this, is the notion of man as essentially a doer or creator, who seeks his good in something that he shares with others, in something of permanent value – in the perfecting of himself and all persons – in self-realization rather than in the pursuit of material well-being.

Human history is for Green the history of the subordination of man's animal self, of the gradual accession of his spiritual nature, his rationalization and moralization. Consequently what distinguishes the proletarian – and to a lesser degree the landlord – is the relative predominance of the animal side of his nature as compared with the capitalist, the subordination of his will for the most part to the passions and inclinations of his sentience; this is what constitutes his underdeveloped consciousness. The individual capitalist too may be characterized by an overriding selfishness; he may engage in practices which are detrimental to the general good. Nevertheless, he is relatively more rational, and more important he is in idea, in possibility, all that man has in him to become – man as self-realizer.

There are, however, two major inconsistencies in Green's theory of human nature. First, his identification of man as self-realizer with capitalist man, as well as his conviction that the true good can be achieved only through the free market system, should not be allowed to obscure his fundamental opposition to certain features of market society. Indeed, it is significant that the animal aspect of Green's man, his 'lower nature,'[46] which is in possibility to be transcended, corresponds quite closely – with one noteworthy exception to be considered presently – to the

---

45 'The Incarnation,' *Works*, III, p. 207
46 PE, sec. 311

classical liberal concept of market man: both are selfish, asocial consumers of utilities. Green's theory of human nature is really an indictment rather than a vindication of market morality.

Similarly, Green's concept of the true good, we have seen, is that it must be non-competitive, 'a good in the effort after which there can be *no* competition between man and man; of which the pursuit of any individual is an equal service to others and to himself.'[47] This is a position, moreover, that Green adopted very early. Commenting on the effects of the market on the literature of his day, he wrote:

Better an old age of poverty and neglect, with five pounds for the poem to keep the poet alive, than a literary life in a time when the intellect is vexed with the spur of competition, and the inspiration of heaven is bargained away in the dearest market. The man of genius may bow in submission to the inseparable accidents of his earthly imprisonment, but he must needs feel the growing burden of an age of intellectual commerce.[48]

Furthermore, Green's objection to the competitive aspects of the market was not confined to their effect upon the literary world. Clearly, he was much more concerned with their impact upon 'the less favoured members of society.' 'They are left to sink or swim' he asserted 'in the stream of unrelenting competition, in which we admit that the weaker has not a chance. So far as negative rights go – rights to be let alone – they are admitted to membership in civil society, but the good things to which the pursuits of society are in fact directed turn out to be no good things for them.'[49]

The problem is that it does not seem possible to reconcile Green's firm opposition to market morality and market behaviour – the egoism, materialism, and competitive struggle – on one hand with his thoroughgoing justification of capitalism and market freedoms on the other. One recent writer, as was noted above, argues that it is not competition as such that is inconsistent with the common good, but 'unrestricted or relentless competition of the sort that increases the powers of some and leaves others with nothing.'[50] Although Cacoullos's suggestion that Green rejects an economic arrangement that 'increases the powers of some and leaves others with nothing' is inaccurate,[51] there is no question that he objects to 'unrestricted or

---

47 PE, sec. 283; emphasis added
48 'The Influence of Civilization on Genius,' *Works*, III, p. 19; cf. p. 18. In a later essay Green moderated somewhat his low opinion of the prevailing literature; but he did not qualify his estimation of competition and the marketplace. 'An Estimate of the Value and Influence of Works of Fiction in Modern Times,' *Works*, III, pp. 44-5
49 PE, sec. 245
50 Ann R. Cacoullos, *Thomas Hill Green: Philosopher of Rights* (New York: Twayne Publishers, 1974), p. 137; cf. pp. 136-8.
51 Her position is based on a misreading of C.B. Macpherson's interpretation of Green (ibid., p. 138).

relentless competition.' The weakness of this view is that Green apparently found *all* competition morally unjustifiable. Green's notion of a non-competitive good and his defence of the market system allows no compromise.[52]

To solve this difficulty, we must note that for Green competition is the product of the pursuit of pleasure. 'The desires, in short, of different men,' he maintains, 'so far as directed each to some pleasure, are *in themselves* tendencies to conflict between man and man.'[53] Similarly, he writes:

Civil society may be, and is, founded on the idea of there being a common good, but that idea in relation to the less favoured members of society is in effect unrealized, and it is unrealized because *the good is being sought in objects which admit of being competed for*. They are of such a kind that they cannot be equally attained by all. The success of some in obtaining them is incompatible with the success of others.[54]

Competition, then, as well as selfishness and the pursuit of pleasure, have their origin in man's animal existence. Green did not see the contradiction in his argument because he saw no necessary connection between market morality, i.e. those norms of human behaviour which have historically been associated with and justified by capitalist market society, and that society itself; market behaviour is for him a state of mind, an underdeveloped consciousness. Like the proletarian, the

52 H.D. Lewis argues that 'Green was obviously under the influence' of the view 'that unrestricted competition would in the long run be to the advantage of all concerned – an advantage understood in terms of material benefit ... It is only because he conceived the rights of men in terms of this principle, in terms of an end which does not, at least very directly, admit of competition, that he was so little occupied with the possibility of an unfair distribution of economic goods resulting from open competition for them.' 'Individualism and Collectivism: A Study of T.H. Green,' in his *Freedom and History* (London: George Allen and Unwin, 1962), pp. 76-7. Like that of Cacoullos, this view attempts to bridge the gap between Green's criticism of competition and his defence of the market system; like Cacoullos's, it is inadequate because the real problem is that Green saw no gap to bridge.

53 PE, sec. 282; emphasis added

54 PE, sec. 245; emphasis added. This quotation reveals the obvious fallacy of Cacoullos's argument that the true good is non-competitive in Green's view because he denied the existence of real scarcity. Cacoullos, *Thomas Hill Green*, p. 138, n. 19.

There is a discrepancy between the last sentence of this passage and Green's earlier contention (PPO, sec. 226) that 'the increased wealth of one man does not necessarily mean the diminished wealth of another,' that 'the wealth of the world is constantly increasing,' and that 'there is nothing [in the private accumulation of wealth] which tends to lessen for anyone else the possibilities of ownership.' Either the present argument is correct, in which case Green is unable to justify unlimited individual appropriation, or the earlier argument is correct, in which case he must give up a persuasive basis of his attack upon the notion of the true good as consisting in pleasure or the means to pleasure. The problem is precisely that Green seeks to maintain both positions at the same time. This contradiction parallels the second major inconsistency to be discussed presently.

egoistic, competitive pleasure-seeker is dominated by his animal nature: he is not adequately conscious of his 'higher' self[55] and thus seeks his good in the satisfaction of his animal appetites. Accordingly, the elimination of such behaviour must entail ultimately man's moralization, the triumph of his spiritual nature over his impulses and inclinations; but the prerequisite of this moralization, we have seen, is the free market system.

This brings us to the second major inconsistency. As C.B. Macpherson has argued, two incompatible concepts of human nature – reducible in the final analysis to the two aspects of Green's model of man – are implied in Green's thought: the first arising from his concept of the true good, the second from his support of market society.[56] In the first place, his theory of the true good implies, in Macpherson's terminology, a concept of man as essentially an exerter and enjoyer of his uniquely human capacities, a concept reflected in Green's notion of man's higher nature. Man, we have seen, realizes himself in creative activity and primarily in his major vocation, his life-work. In so far as this vocation is the one for which he is best suited, it will represent both his greatest personal good and his greatest possible contribution to mankind.

In order to realize this good, however, the individual requires access to the instruments of his work, the means of labour. Thus, Green rejects the classical liberal notion of property as merely a means to the acquisition of pleasure. He affirms instead that 'the moral functions of property'[57] consist in the provision of the means of self-expression and self-fulfilment and in serving as 'a permanent apparatus for carrying out a plan of life.'[58] As a matter of course, Green stipulates, there will be inequality of property, but only such as results naturally from the free and unimpeded exercise of diverse human talents. 'The rationale of property' he points out 'is that *everyone* should be secured in the power of getting and keeping *the means of realizing a will*, which in possibility is a will directed to social good.'[59]

Because man is an exerter and developer of his capacities, all persons are entitled to equal access to the means of labour. Thus Green defines 'the ideal of true freedom' as 'the maximum of power for *all* members of human society *alike* to make the best of themselves.'[60] The good, moreover, cannot be achieved by some at the

55 'The Word is Nigh Thee,' *Works*, III, p. 223
56 C.B. Macpherson, *Democratic Theory: Essays in Retrieval* (Oxford: at the Clarendon Press, 1973), pp. 4-12, 24-36. Cf. Phillip Hansen, 'T.H. Green and the Moralization of the Market.' *Canadian Journal of Political and Social Theory*, I: No. 1 (Winter, 1977), pp. 100-4, 108-9.
57 PPO, sec. 226
58 PPO, sec. 220
59 PPO, sec. 221; emphasis added
60 'Liberal Legislation,' *Works*, III, p. 372; emphasis added. On the same page Green defines true or positive freedom as 'the liberation of the powers of *all* men *equally* for contributions to a common good' and refers to 'that *equal* development of the faculties of *all* which is the highest good of all.' Emphasis added

expense of others; 'we rightly refuse to recognize the highest development on the part of an exceptional individual or exceptional class' he maintains 'as an advance towards the true freedom of man, if it is founded on a refusal of the same opportunity to other men.'[61]

At the same time, according to Macpherson, Green's contention that the capitalist market system is the sine qua non of the actualization of the true good implies his acceptance of the Hobbes-to-Bentham model of man as essentially an infinite consumer and appropriator, a model reflected in Green's notion of the lower nature of man. However, the organization of society in such a way as to fulfil this concept of human nature, with the legitimization of the right of unlimited individual appropriation (a right Green himself recognized), leads inevitably to the private appropriation of all available land and capital, leaving the majority of persons without free access to the means of labour. To gain such access they must sell their labour, that is, transfer some of their powers, to the owners of the instruments of production. The outcome of such an arrangement is not, as Green envisaged, 'the liberation of the powers of *all* men *equally* for contributions to a common good,'[62] but rather the continuous net transfer of powers from the non-owners to the owners of land and capital, and the unequal possibility therefore of non-owners of property, as compared with owners, to develop themselves – the creation, in short, 'of a proletariate, practically excluded from such ownership as is needed to moralize a man.'[63] The class divisions of his society were not, as Green believed, the manifestation of different levels of consciousness, but the necessary and inexorable product of capitalist relations of production. Moreover, the two concepts of man implicit in Green's system, like the two aspects of his model of human nature, are conflicting and mutually exclusive.[64]

This contradiction in Green's thought also emerges as an inconsistency within the concept of the spiritual nature of man itself. It was suggested above that the animal side of man corresponds quite closely to the liberal model of man with one important difference; the difference is that, according to Green, man, in his animal aspect, is not an *infinite* appropriator. Man appropriates by virtue of his higher self. The acquisition of permanent possessions implies, for Green, that man is other and more than a merely sentient being, that he shares a community of spirit with the eternal mind.[65] In addition, this notion underlies Green's belief that the underdeveloped

61 Ibid., p. 371
62 Ibid., p. 372; emphasis added
63 PPO, sec. 222
64 On Macpherson's concept of the 'transfer of powers' see his *Democratic Theory: Essays in Retrieval*, pp. 10-18, 34-5, 40-1, 64-6; *The Political Theory of Possessive Individualism: Hobbes to Locke* (Oxford: at the Clarendon Press, 1962), pp. 55-7; and *The Real World of Democracy* (Toronto: CBC Publications, 1965), pp. 40-5.
65 Cf. J.H. Muirhead, *The Service of the State* (London: John Murray, 1908), p. 76.

consciousness of the proletariat is the chief cause of their propertyless condition. It is, moreover, as a function of his spiritual nature that man appropriates (and desires) *infinitely*, for his insatiability appears to stem from his consciousness of himself as permanent or eternal, as outlasting his present appetites, and as seeing his good as including the satisfaction of the needs of others.[66]

The very concept of the spiritual nature of man is therefore internally inconsistent. Furthermore, since self-realizing man is dominated by his higher self, Green's identification of man as self-realizer, man as exerter and developer of his capacities, with capitalist man stripped of some of his more unsavoury characteristics is ultimately self-defeating. Green did not see the self-contradiction of his position because he did not see that historically the same market man as infinite appropriator is necessarily selfish, materialistic, and competitive, that infinite appropriation is a function of man's lower, animal consciousness. Accordingly, to equate man as self-realizer with bourgeois man, to argue that market society is a precondition of the true good, is upon Green's own principles logically untenable.

4

Both those contradictions went unnoticed by Green because he failed to perceive the social foundations of his model of human nature. This error led him to argue both that market morality could be transcended in a society dominated by a capitalist market economy and that such a society is necessary for the perfecting of man, to argue that certain characteristics of market man are the negation, and certain others the expression, of man's nature as self-realizer.

In general, Green underestimated the extent to which social conditions determine human nature. One of his fundamental principles, we have seen, was that man is self-determining, a 'free cause'; human consciousness, he maintained, transcends social conditions. Thus he conceived of man's animal nature as simply a manifestation of his existence as a physical, sentient being and consequently as independent of determination by social forces. In like manner he viewed man's spiritual nature as the product of the divine mind reproducing itself in man, and hence as similarly independent.

Indeed, Green himself *denies* the duality of his model of man, thereby drawing sceptical responses from some commentators.[67] While he traces his concept of

---

66 'If we leave a man free to realize the conception of a possible well-being, it is impossible to limit the effect upon him of his desire to provide for his future well-being as including that of the persons in whom he is interested.' PPO, sec. 223. Cf. John Rodman, 'What is Living and What is Dead in the Political Philosophy of T.H. Green,' *Western Political Quarterly*, XXVI: No. 3 (Sept. 1973), pp. 578-9.

67 See John Dewey, 'Green's Theory of the Moral Motive,' *Philosophical Review*, I: No. 6, Whole No. 6 (Nov. 1892), pp. 597-600; and his 'Self-Realization as the Moral Ideal,' pp. 661-3; Oskar

human nature to Kant, he rejects, in no uncertain terms, the basic duality of Kant's man, much as he rejected the dualisms of feeling and thought, of phenomenon and noumenon.[68] The notion of two exclusive and incompatible sides of human nature, of an empirical and an intelligible character, is for Green basically without meaning. 'We have not two minds' he maintains 'but one mind.' The true explanation of the matter is

not that there is a double consciousness, but that the one indivisible reality of our consciousness cannot be comprehended in a single conception. In seeking to understand its reality we have to look at it from two different points of view; and the different conceptions that we form of it, as looked at from these different points, do not admit of being united, any more than do our impressions of opposite sides of the same shield.[69]

In effect, Green is arguing that the two natures of man he has described are merely two stages in a process of development: man's original, natural state and his real or possible self.[70] Looking at man at any historical moment will thus yield a 'mixed' nature, which must be dissected to be fully comprehended. Despite his protestations, however, Green has described two selves, two natures, two states of consciousness, that are fundamentally and irretrievably incompatible. They are not two stages in a continuous process of development; each, rather, implies the negation of the other.

To be sure, the notion of a divided, self-contradictory human nature is not new. Indeed, Green himself thought he was describing the absolute, immutable nature of

Günther, *Das Verhältnis der Ethik Thomas Hill Greens zu derjenigen Kants* (PHD dissertation, Dresden: Theodor Beyer, 1915), pp. 54-5; Rudolf Metz, *A Hundred Years of British Philosophy*, transl. by J.W. Harvey, T.E. Jessop and Henry Sturt, ed. by J.H. Muirhead (London: George Allen and Unwin, 1950), pp. 278-9; and, Henry Sturt, *Idola Theatri* (London: Macmillan, 1906), pp. 238-9. Cf. Isaiah Berlin, *Two Concepts of Liberty*, in *Four Essays on Liberty* (New York: Oxford University Press, 1969), pp. 131-4.

Other commentators, however, have accepted Green's denial at face value. See, for example, W.G. de Burgh, 'Self-Realization,' *Hibbert Journal*, XXVI (July 1928), p. 688; Cacoullos, *Thomas Hill Green*, pp. 46-7, 57-8; Edward Caird, 'Professor Green's Last Work,' *Mind*, VIII: No. 32 (Oct. 1883), pp. 545-6, 559; H.D. Lewis, 'Some Observations on Natural Rights and the General Will (II),' *Mind*, New Series, XLVII: No. 185 (Jan. 1938), pp. 18-9; Jean Pucelle, *L'Idéalisme en Angleterre: De Coleridge à Bradley* (Neuchatel: Editions de la Baconnière, 1955), pp. 146-7, 150. Cf. also Nettleship, 'Memoir,' *Works*, III, pp. cxxxiii-cxxxiv.

68 See *Lectures on Kant*, sec. 4; and PE, secs 30, 39, 41, 51.

69 PE, sec. 68. Cf. *Lectures on Kant*, secs 84 (addition), 86, 87, 92, 93; and 'On the Different Senses of "Freedom,"' *Works*, II, secs 20, 21, 22. Although Green rejects Kant's notion of the heteronomy vs the autonomy of the will, he merely replaces it with his two concepts of freedom: *all* persons are free, though they may be dominated solely by their animal natures; only those are *truly* free, however, whose wills are governed by their spiritual natures.

70 In Green's view, however, man never has and never will conform entirely to either nature.

man. He saw the opposition in man as a struggle between eternal, universal truths: between the spirit and the flesh, virtue and vice, good and evil. His particular application of this analysis to the people and conditions of nineteenth-century England, however, indicates an obvious historical and social bias. Green's concept of human nature justifies the capitalist market and its freedoms, including the right of unlimited private appropriation, attributes the existence of a proletariat to causes wholly unrelated to the market system, and views bourgeois man as the quintessence of human development; it does all this in spite of the incompatibility between capitalism and his theory of self-realization.

What, then, is the significance of Green's theory of a dichotomous human nature? What led him to perceive the transformation of human consciousness as a moral imperative? I suggest that, contrary to his own conviction, Green's theory of human nature depicts not universal man but bourgeois man and in particular reflects the alienation of man in industrial capitalist society. His model of human nature portrays man as having two opposite aspects, as internally divided, simply because it portrays market man.

Not that the 'one-dimensional' Hobbes-to-Bentham model of man did not accurately depict bourgeois man. On the contrary, it had been and continued to be in Green's time an accurate representation of how the members of a market society behave. However, changing social and economic conditions had created new possibilities for human development and the need to view man in a different perspective. Green, writing at least fifty years after Bentham and a full two centuries after Hobbes, was able to identify these possibilities and this perspective but without being aware of their historical implications.

By the time of Green's earliest systematic formulation of his social and political thought in the 1860s, the industrialization of the English economy had been proceeding for more than a century. Man was fast developing the productive forces that might eliminate natural scarcity, and the technological means to liberate him from arduous, time-consuming toil. For the first time man had become potentially a truly social being, whose personal good is a contribution to the general well-being, an end-in-himself, a realizer and developer of his unique capacities. At the same time, the market system, which required man to be a selfish, insatiable appropriator, was becoming an ever-greater obstacle to the actualization of man's new-found possibilities.

If allowance is made for those errors in Green's analysis arising from his social assumptions, man's lower nature, his actual self, corresponds to market man; his higher nature, his possible self, represents *post*-market man. Green's concept of human nature, in short, reflects the alienation of the men and women of his time, citizens of advanced market society. The transformation of human consciousness he envisaged was necessary to the overcoming of this alienation, to the fulfilment of human capabilities, and to 'the liberation of the powers of all men equally for contributions to a common good.'

One further assumption implied in Green's thought substantiates this interpretation. Since the dual nature of man is for Green the result not of social forces but of the immutable circumstances of human life, the divided, self-contradictory nature of man is for him the human condition; ultimately man can escape neither his physical limitations nor his spiritual heritage. Self-realization, the true end of all human endeavour, is never fully attainable, for such is the nature of human existence.

Green's resignation to the fact of the duality of the human condition, his acceptance of man's alienation as unalterable, constitutes an implicit acceptance of the limitations on human development unavoidably imposed by market society. What Green did not see – but what his system implicitly recognizes – is that a transformation of human consciousness is not possible without a corresponding transformation in the social and economic conditions of human existence. Without the latter, man's nature as a self-realizer must remain unfulfilled, shackled and constrained by his lower, market nature.

7

The critique of utilitarianism

At the outset of this study it was suggested that a primary aim of Green's undertaking was to provide a new theoretical foundation for the values and institutions of nineteenth-century England, to explain the changes and upheavals his society was experiencing, and to indicate a course of action to weather the storm. This function was not, he believed, being adequately performed by the dominant philosophical system of his day, the revised utilitarianism of John Stuart Mill, which according to Green was founded on an inaccurate interpretation of human behaviour and motivation and was itself inconsistent with its theoretical base:

Even the English epicureanism has felt the change. To its formula of the 'greatest happiness,' as the object of the moral life, it has added, 'of the greatest number.' If this be construed (as, to secure consistency, it must be) to mean merely that the individual, in living for his own pleasure, is to take account of the pleasure of others as the condition of his own, it is, of course, no essential modification of the doctrine of Hume. But the modern English Utilitarian is generally better than his logic. In defiance of Hume and Bentham, he distinguishes higher and lower pleasures by some other criterion than that of quantity, and takes as the object to which 'expediency' is relative a 'good of others,' which involves his own. He is not practically the worse for failing to perceive that to live for such an object is to live, not for the attainment of any sum of agreeable sensations, but for the realization of an idea, of which the philosophy that starts from feeling can give no account.[1]

It is now possible to examine in detail Green's critique of utilitarian moral philosophy, in its classical hedonistic expression as well as in its amended version. What this critique reveals, above all, is Green's fundamental misunderstanding of

---

1 'Popular Philosophy in its Relation to Life,' *Works*, III, p. 124; cf. PE, sec. 162. Elsewhere, Green refers to 'that hybrid, though beneficent, utilitarianism which finds the moral good in the "greatest happiness of the greatest number."' *Hume II*, sec. 64

the nature and limits of utilitarianism as the justificatory theory of capitalist market society, a misunderstanding based in the final analysis on the contradiction, discussed in the last chapter, between Green's concept of self-realization and his vindication of the major institutions of the capitalist market economy.[2]

I

Green's critique of utilitarianism as a system of ethics takes the form of an assault, on a number of levels, upon the logical foundations of the utilitarian moral edifice. Utilitarianism, he maintains, is unable to provide an adequate moral criterion, a standard against which the virtue or vice of human activity might be measured. It is self-evident, according to Green, although we shall have reason to question this claim, 'that the possibility of moral judgments implies some idea of a good, other than any particular pleasure or satisfaction of passing desire, with the superior value of which the value of any such pleasure or satisfaction may be compared.' Thus if, as utilitarianism postulates, man is assumed to be by nature a desirer of pleasure, 'we are apt to look upon the idea of a superior good as formed merely by the combination in thought of the many particular pleasures and satisfactions, as an imagined sum of them.'[3] The *summum bonum*, that is to say, is likely to be regarded as the greatest possible sum of pleasures.

But the true good as so conceived is in Green's view ultimately unserviceable as a moral standard. 'Pleasures' he contends 'do not admit of being accumulated in enjoyment.'[4] 'Pleasant feelings are not quantities that can be added. Each is over before the next begins, and the man who has been pleased a million times is not really better off – has no more of the supposed chief good in his possession – than the man who has been pleased a thousand times.'[5] Thus there cannot be a sum of pleasures as pleasures, but only as 'addible quantities.'[6] 'It is only as counted, not as enjoyed, that they accumulate, and when we speak of them as together constituting

2 In this chapter my remarks and arguments are confined to that tradition of utilitarianism with which Green was himself concerned, the moral system that formed the underpinning of eighteenth- and nineteenth-century British liberalism and was most clearly represented in the works of Bentham and the Mills. It is not my intention, therefore, to suggest that utilitarian arguments cannot be (or have not been) used to justify some other form of social arrangement, although in the hands of Bentham and the Mills it was most certainly a justificatory theory of the market system; similarly, I do not wish to suggest that utilitarian grounds could not be called upon to justify change (even revolutionary change) in the status quo. However, the extent to which utilitarianism can successfully serve such a role is beyond the scope of the present study.

3 PE, sec. 221; cf. sec. 220.

4 PE, sec. 227

5 *Hume II*, sec. 7. Cf. *Hume I*, sec. 258; and 'Note on Henry Sidwick's "Hedonism and Ultimate Good,"' *Mind*, II: No. 6 (April 1877), p. 267 (hereinafter cited as 'Note on Sidgwick').

6 PE, sec. 221

the chief good, we are confusing a sum of numeration with a sum of coexistence or enjoyment.'[7]

Second, if, to remove the difficulty, the greatest possible sum of pleasures is defined – not as a sum, implying coexistence – but as the greatest possible series or succession of pleasures, the result is of no appreciable assistance. Since pleasures, as sensations, pass as soon as they are felt, there is no effective difference between the true good as a mere succession of pleasures, i.e. as being pleased again and again ad infinitum, and the true good as being pleased once. Green concludes:

Thus to the person who says that the greatest sum of pleasures is the chief good we may offer two alternatives. Either the subject of his proposition is (as a German might say) an *Unding* or the predicate is inappropriate. If by the 'sum of pleasures' he means an accumulation of pleasures for consciousness, the absurdity lies in the subject of the proposition. Though, if there could be such a thing, there might be sense in calling it the chief good, there can be no such thing. If, on the other hand, by the 'greatest sum of pleasures' he means the being pleased as often as possible without implication of any coexistence of pleasures, he is giving sense to the subject of his proposition at the expense of what he predicates of it. There is no ground for distinction between the sum of pleasures, thus understood, as the *chief* good and any particular pleasure as good. The moral criterion has disappeared.[8]

Furthermore, since pleasures cannot be accumulated, a sum of pleasures is not itself a feeling of pleasure. Accordingly, Green reasons, although there may be a sense in which a sum of pleasures could conceivably constitute the true good, it cannot serve this purpose in the utilitarian system, which portrays man as a desirer of pleasures: 'If desire is only for pleasure, i.e. for an enjoyment or feeling of pleasure, we are simply the victims of words when we talk of desire for a sum of pleasures, much more when we take the greatest imaginable sum to be the most desired.'[9] Green continues:

it is not intended to deny that there may be in fact such a thing as desire for a sum or contemplated series of pleasures, or that a man may be so affected by it as to judge that some particular desire should not be gratified, if its gratification would interfere with the attainment of that more desirable object. The contention is merely that there could not be such a desire if desire were solely for pleasure, in the sense of being always excited by an imagination of some feeling of pleasure. As there cannot be a feeling of a sum of pleasures, neither can there be an imagination of such a feeling. Desire for a sum or series of pleasures is only possible so

7 'Note on Sidgwick,' p. 269
8 Ibid.
9 PE, sec. 221

far as upon sundry desires, each excited by imagination of a particular pleasure, there super-venes in a man a desire not excited by any such imagination; a desire for self-satisfaction ... Thus, in order to account for the transition from desire for imagined pleasures to desire for a sum or series of pleasures, we must suppose the action of a principle wholly different from desire for imagined pleasures. We must suppose a determination of desire by the conception of self, its direction to self-satisfaction.[10]

To be capable of desiring a sum of pleasures, in other words, man, in Green's estimation, must be more than a mere desirer of pleasures: he must be conscious of himself as a permanent subject, 'as there to be satisfied when any feeling, in the enjoyment of which he may have sought satisfaction, is over.'[11] In that case he would indeed be capable of seeking his true good in a greatest possible sum of pleasures, but it is highly doubtful, Green asserts, that he would in fact seek it in such an end. 'A desire to satisfy oneself, then, as distinct from desire for a feeling of pleasure, being necessary even to desire for a sum of pleasures, the question is whether it can be a contemplated possibility of satisfying oneself *with pleasures* that yields the idea of a true or higher good, with which particular gratifications of desire may be contrasted.'[12]

Green believed, moreover, not merely that the possibility of the desire for a sum of pleasures implies, on the part of the individual, a conception of a self to be satisfied but also that the very capacity of forming any moral judgment whatsoever implies such a conception:

For an agent merely capable of seeking the satisfaction of successive desires, without capa-city for conceiving a satisfaction of himself as other than the satisfaction of any particular desire, and in consequence without capacity for conceiving anything as good permanently or on the whole, there could be no possibility of judging that any desire should or should not be gratified. No such judgment can be formed of any desire, unless the desire is considered with reference to a good other than such as passes with the satisfaction of a desire. Even if the judgment involved no more than a comparison of the pleasures that had been experienced in the gratification of different desires, and a decision that one should not be gratified because interfering with the gratification of another from which more pleasure was expected, this very comparison would imply that the person making it distinguished himself from his desires and was cognizant of something good for himself on the whole – though for himself only in respect of his capacity for pleasure – to which good he expects the gratification of one desire to contribute more than that of another.[13]

10 PE, sec. 222
11 PE, sec. 223
12 PE, sec. 222; cf. secs 227, 228.
13 PE, sec. 220

'Our conclusion then' Green argues 'is that it is a misinterpretation of consciousness ... to regard the idea of a true or higher good, with which the good of any particular pleasure or the gratification of any particular passion may be contrasted – an idea necessary to the capacity for moral judgment – as equivalent or reducible to the idea of a larger sum of pleasures enjoyable by the person entertaining the idea.'[14]

What, then, is the source of this 'misinterpretation of consciousness'? Why are individuals so easily persuaded that their greatest good lies in the greatest possible sum of pleasures, a notion Green describes as 'intrinsically nonsense'?[15] While it is true, he admits, that individuals may and do seek self-satisfaction in pleasure, it is equally true that more often than not the object of desire is something other than pleasure, to the attainment of which, however, pleasure is normally attendant because the desiring individual has found, or believes himself to have found, satisfaction. 'Ordinary motives' he contends 'are interests in the attainment of objects, without which it seems to the man in his actual state that he cannot satisfy himself, and in attaining which, because he has desired them, he will find a certain pleasure, but only because he previously desired them, not because pleasures are the objects desired.'[16] The belief, therefore, that pleasure is 'the sole object of desire,' that the greatest possible sum of pleasures constitutes the true good, results, according to Green, from 'a confusion between the object which excites desire and the pleasure which ensues upon the satisfaction of the desire; in other words, the mistake of supposing that desire is excited by the anticipation of its own satisfaction; whereas, obviously, desire must previously have been excited by some other object before any such satisfaction can be anticipated.'[17] It is desire for an object that determines the pleasure that will follow upon its realization, not the imagination of pleasure that determines the desire.

Green, however, recognizing the hold of utilitarianism on the minds of his contemporaries, is not content to let matters rest there. Granting for the sake of argument the legitimacy of the notion of the greatest possible sum of pleasures, he still finds it unavailable as a moral criterion. Because utilitarianism assumes that an individual in any given instance will necessarily act in such a way as to get as much pleasure as is attainable by him, it is logically impermissible to judge that he should or should not have acted as he did. Utilitarianism can only lead to what he terms 'Hedonistic fatalism'[18]:

14 PE, sec. 229; cf. *Hume II*, secs 5, 14.
15 'Note on Sidgwick,' p. 269
16 PE, sec. 160
17 *Lectures on Kant*, sec. 119. See also sec. 123; and PE, secs 158, 159, 161, 167, 168, 171, 219, 223, 224, 337, 361.
18 PE, secs 351, 374; see also sec. 350.

The Utilitarian who does not probe his Hedonistic principles to the bottom has no difficulty in saying of any one that he ought to do what he does not, because, while he takes for granted that the largest balance of possible pleasure is the chief good, he does not question that it is open to the man who 'does what he ought not' to obtain a larger quantity of pleasure for himself and for others than he in fact obtains by acting as he does. But upon Hedonistic principles ... it is clearly not possible for a man, as his desires and aversions at any time stand, to obtain at the time by his own act more pleasure, or avoid more pain, than he in fact does. We cannot therefore, consistently with these principles, tell the man whom we count vicious that, according to the common Utilitarian language, he wilfully disregards his own true interest and throws away his own greatest happiness.[19]

Although it might appear legitimate in many cases, he adds, to urge upon utilitarian principles that an individual would have obtained greater pleasure, or that the members of society as a whole might have had greater pleasure, had he acted in a different manner, such a judgment is in the final analysis impossible to support. The determination of pleasure depends very much on the individual instance, and the variables are too numerous and too complicated to allow any certain conclusions.[20]

The only 'morality' consistently deducible from utilitarian assumptions is that dictated, not by any desire on the part of an individual to improve himself, but by 'the interest of the stronger.'[21] Since the individual will always seek his greatest pleasure, Green reasons, his judgment that he ought to act differently implies that he is acting against his own natural inclinations, that he is acting in accordance with the determination by some other person or persons of where his greatest pleasure is to be found:

Thus the consciousness 'I ought to do this or that' must be interpreted as equivalent to the consciousness that it is expected of me by others, who are 'stronger' than I am in the sense that they have power to reward or punish me – whether these 'others' are represented by the civil magistrate or by some public opinion, whether the rewards and punishments proceeding from them are in the nature of what we call physical, or what we call mental, pleasure and pain. It is their interest which is the ultimate foundation of the judgment, on the part of the individual, that he ought or ought not.[22]

It is true, Green asserts, that the 'stronger' tends historically to become the majority, so that 'the morally better for any member of that society will be the greatest

---

19 PE, sec. 341; cf. secs 340, 343, 346, 347, 356. This is also expressed by Green as the absence of a distinction between the 'desired' and the 'desirable,' i.e. between what the individual actually desires and what he should desire. Cf. PE, sec. 168.
20 PE, secs 341, 342, 343; cf. 'Note on Sidgwick,' p. 268.
21 PE, sec. 347
22 PE, sec. 348; cf. sec. 349.

pleasure of the greatest number.'[23] 'But' he continues 'as there is no fixedness or
finality either in the ruling influence of society, or in the modes of action which those
who exercise this influence find most for their pleasure, no final or absolute judgment can be given as to the morally better or worse.'[24]

Finally, he suggests, even if one allows that utilitarianism – by dissociating it
from the hedonistic theory of motives, i.e. from the concept of man as a mere desirer
of pleasure – is able to provide a moral criterion, and even if that criterion consists
in the greatest possible sum of pleasures, utilitarianism must yet lose 'what has been
in fact its chief claim to the acceptance of ordinary men,'[25] that is, its clarity and
precision as an instrument for calculating human morality. Indeed, he argues, the
greatest possible sum of pleasures turns out to be a rather indefinite and immeasur-
able quantity, because since men must continue to acquire pleasures as long as they
live it appears impossible that there can be 'any such greatest sum as can satisfy the
conception.'[26] 'To say that ultimate good is a greatest possible sum of pleasures,
strictly taken, is to say that it is an end which for ever recedes; which is not only
unattainable but from the nature of the case can never be more nearly approached;
and such an end clearly cannot serve the purpose of a criterion, by enabling us to
distinguish actions which bring men nearer to it from those that do not.'[27]

If the notion of a greatest possible sum of pleasures is therefore not a definite
quantity, what is it? According to Green, since it cannot refer to a numerical sum, it
must rather be taken to indicate 'a certain state of existence':

The reason why [the utilitarian] approves an action is not that he judges it likely to make an
addition to a sum of pleasures which never comes nearer completion, but that he judges it
likely to contribute to this state of general enjoyable existence. If he says that the right object
for a man is to increase the stock of human enjoyments, it is presumable that he is not really
thinking of an addition to a sum of pleasant experiences, however large, which might be
made and yet leave those who had had the experiences with no more of the good in possession
than they had before. He does not mean that a thousand experiences of pleasure constitute
more of a good than nine hundred experiences of the same intensity, or less of a good than six
hundred of a double intensity. He is thinking of a good consisting in a certain sort of social
life, of which he does not particularize the nature to himself further than by conceiving it as a
pleasant life to all who share in it, and as one of which all have the enjoyment, if not equally
yet none at the cost of others.[28]

23 PE, sec. 348
24 PE, sec. 349
25 PE, sec. 357
26 PE, sec. 360
27 PE, sec. 359
28 PE, sec. 360

As a result, the notion of the true good as consisting in the greatest possible sum of pleasures, 'instead of having that definiteness which, because all know what pleasure is, it seemed at first to promise ... turns out on consideration to be so abstract and indefinite.'[29]

This, then, is the substance of Green's critique of the utilitarian system before its revision by J.S. Mill. As we have seen, he virtually denies to utilitarianism any validity either as an adequate explanation of how men do behave or as a possible guide to how they should behave. Nevertheless, he acknowledges, 'there is no doubt that the theory of an ideal good, consisting in the greatest happiness of the greatest number, as the end by reference to which the claim of all laws and powers and rules of action on our obedience is to be tested, has tended to improve human conduct and character.'[30] But the beneficial practical effects of utilitarianism cannot in his view be attributed to its theoretical analysis:

The practical service, however, thus rendered by utilitarianism has been independent of its analysis of well-being or good. It has been by insisting that it is 'the greatest number' whose highest good is to be taken into account, not by identifying that highest good with a greatest nett quantity of pleasure, that it has improved the organization of human life. It is thus that it has given a wider and more impartial range to public spirit, to the desire to do good.[31]

Utilitarianism has thus been a major moralizing influence in modern society, but not because of its concept of man as a desirer of pleasure. This influence has been because it has espoused the equality of all men, 'because it has most definitely announced the interest of humanity, without distinction of persons or classes, as the end by reference to which all claims upon obedience are ultimately to be measured ... Impartiality of reference to human well-being has been the great lesson which the utilitarian has had to teach.'[32] There is in fact no necessary connection, Green maintains, between this lesson and the utilitarian philosophy of morals; 'in most cases where a man has to decide how he may best promote the greatest good of others, it makes little practical difference in regard to the line of action to be taken, whether he considers their greatest good to lie in the possession of a certain character, as an end not a means, or in the enjoyment of the most pleasure of which they are capable.'[33]

29 PE, sec. 361
30 PE, sec. 331
31 PE, sec. 332
32 PE, sec. 333
33 PE, sec. 332. Green makes essentially the same point in a brief, earlier discussion of Bentham's
    'formula, that "every one should count for one and no one for more than one" in the calculation

2

Before evaluating Green's critique of utilitarianism, I shall consider briefly Green's treatment of J.S. Mill's moral system. Although it forms only a very small portion of his general critique of utilitarianism, it nevertheless concerns what Green himself considers an extremely significant matter, Mill's departure from Benthamite utilitarianism:

[Mill], as is well known, differs from the older Utilitarians in holding that, although pleasure and freedom from pain are the only things desirable as ends, some *kinds* of pleasure are more desirable and valuable than others, not as involving a greater amount of pleasure, but in their intrinsic nature. Every one must feel that the Utilitarian theory receives a certain exaltation from his treatment of it, and especially from his assertion of this point. But the question is whether the admissions which he has to make in order to establish it do not virtually amount to a departure from the doctrine that pleasure or freedom from pain is the only object of desire.[34]

The importance for Green of Mill's revision of utilitarianism, is that it supplies a moral criterion that the classical expression of utilitarianism was unable to provide. In so far as the objects of desire are distinguishable as higher or lower, as qualitatively more or less valuable, the moral judgment that a certain object ought to be desired, or that a certain course of action ought to be pursued, has a significance which, Green contends, cannot attach to it upon the assumption that all desire is for pleasure: Though I am, in a sense, 'naturally' inclined to desire the lower objects, I am somehow 'better,' I improve myself, in proportion as I desire objects of the higher type; therefore, I ought to desire them. Although Green is in substantial agreement with Mill's conclusions, however, he finds them to be based on faulty premises.

---

of felicific consequences.' This, he remarks, is the basis of utilitarianism's 'real beneficence in the life of modern society' (PE, sec. 213). At the same time, however, he is less kind here than in the later context, because strictly speaking, he argues, it is not persons who are supposed equal but their susceptibility to pleasure. 'Now as the ascertainment of this equality in degree between the happiness of one man and that of another is practically impossible, and as there is every reason to think that different men are susceptible of pleasure in different degrees, it is hard to see how the formula, thus interpreted, can afford any positive ground for that treatment of all men's happiness as entitled to equal consideration, for which Utilitarians have in practice been so laudably zealous.' Moreover, he suggests that in accordance with such a theory 'a superior race or order could plead strong justification, not indeed for causing useless pain to the inferior, but for systematically postponing the inferior's claims to happiness to his own' (PE, sec. 214).

34 PE, sec. 162

According to Green, if pleasure is the sole object of desire, there can be no intrinsic difference in the nature of the objects of desire: they all must consist either in pleasure or in the removal of pain.[35] Thus, whether I desire pushpin or poetry, my object – what I desire – is pleasure, plain and simple, and there is no ground for distinction between the one object and the other except in the amount of pleasure I may obtain. 'The strict Benthamites' he maintains 'hold that such differences of kind between pleasures as arise from differences in their exciting causes only affect their value or the degree of their goodness, in so far as they affect the amount of pleasure enjoyed on the whole; while Mill holds that these differences affect the value of pleasures independently of the effect they have on their amount. The estimation of pleasures should not depend on quantity alone: quality is to be considered as well as quantity.'[36]

Mill's contention cannot therefore be consistently maintained in view of his own acceptance of the principle that all desire is for pleasure. Given this assumption, no object can be deemed of greater intrinsic value, no person can be deemed as somehow 'better in himself' for desiring such an object. 'On this principle' Green writes 'one man can be better, one faculty higher than another, only as a more serviceable instrument for the production of pleasure.' Nor does the evidence Mill adduces, that individuals who have experienced both higher and lower pleasures prefer the former, answer Green's objection:

If we rid ourselves then of all presuppositions, illegitimate on Utilitarian principles, in regard to the superiority of the man or the faculties exercised in what we call the highest pursuits, and if we admit that all desire is for pleasure, the strongest desire for the greatest pleasure, what is proved by the example of the man who, being 'competently acquainted with both,' prefers the life of moral and intellectual effort to one of healthy animal enjoyment? Simply this, that the life of effort brings more pleasure to the man in question than *he* would derive from the other sort of life. It outweighs for him any quantity of other pleasure *of which his nature is capable* ... The example of a certain man's preference, unless we have some other standard of his excellence than such as is relative to pleasure as the ultimate good, proves nothing as to the superiority of the pleasure which he chooses to another sort of pleasure preferred by some one else. It only proves that it is more of a pleasure *to him* than is that to which he prefers it.[37]

What, then, is the source of Mill's error? How could he have argued both that the sole object of desire is pleasure and that some objects are qualitatively better than

35 *Lectures on Kant*, sec. 119
36 PE, sec. 163; cf. sec. 156.
37 PE, sec. 164; Green's emphasis. Cf. secs 165, 166.

others? The problem, Green urges, is the confusion, previously encountered, between pleasure as the object of desire and that pleasure which accompanies the satisfaction of desire, though the desire be for some object other than pleasure:

The real ground then of Mill's departure from the stricter Utilitarian doctrine, that the worth of pleasure depends simply on its amount, is his virtual surrender of the doctrine that all desire is for pleasure; but he does not recognize this surrender, because he thinks that to call a desired object part of the happiness of the person desiring it is equivalent to saying that the desire for the object is a desire for pleasure.[38]

Indeed, Green asserts, Mill virtually admits that desire may be for objects other than pleasure, for he suggests that such things as money, power, fame, and virtue, though originally desired as means to pleasure, have come to be desired as ends in themselves. To be sure, Green acknowledges, they are desired, according to Mill, as elements in the individual's conception of his happiness. Nevertheless, they are themselves not pleasures. 'If money, fame, and power are desired not as a means to pleasure but for their own sake – and this Mill admits – then there are desires, whatever their history, which are not desires for pleasures, however essential their gratification may be to the happiness of those who desire.'[39]

3

It is now possible to assess the implications of Green's critique of utilitarianism for his own work. The major points of his critique are as follows:

(i) The very possibility of moral judgments implies some idea of a true good, 'other than any particular pleasure or satisfaction of passing desire,' to serve as a moral criterion. (Mill's attempt to supply a moral criterion through the postulate of different qualities of pleasure is, according to Green, logically unfounded.)
(ii) The notion of a greatest possible sum of pleasures is intrinsically unavailable for this purpose, because a sum of pleasures is not itself a pleasure.
(iii) In so far as man is able to desire a sum of pleasures, he is not a mere desirer of pleasure. In fact, any notion of a true good requires a conception of self as other than one's desires and thus implies that man is more than a mere desirer of pleasure.
(iv) Pleasure is not the sole object of desire. It is not pleasure (or the imagination of pleasure) that determines desire, but desire that determines ensuing pleasure. (It is

38 PE, sec. 167; cf. secs 162, 165, 168, 169.
39 PE, sec. 169; cf. sec. 170. For Green's critique of Sidgwick's 'Universalistic Hedonism,' see PE, secs 364-74.

Mill's failure to recognize this principle, in Green's view, that accounts for his confusion.)

(v) Granting that the greatest possible pleasure is the true good, utilitarianism must lead to 'hedonistic fatalism': since an individual *always* acts so as to obtain his greatest possible pleasure, there is no possibility of moral judgment nor a reason for moral improvement.

(vi) Granting that utilitarianism may be independent of the hedonistic theory of motives, the greatest possible sum of pleasures is not a definite, measurable quantity, but a state of existence.

(vii) Equality is not a necessary or logical implication of utilitarianism.

The argument in (i) constitutes a defence of the non-market notion of an absolute good, of a true and eternal good as determined by a higher, non-natural force. Market morality, on the contrary, finds the good originating in the needs and dictates of human nature: that which satisfies this nature is good; that which the market determines is just. There is in this view no higher morality than that of the natural human impulses, and indeed it is precisely bourgeois man who is incapable of any higher concept of morality, such as that implied by (iii). While Green also claims to derive his notion of the true good as the only adequate moral criterion from the needs and capacities of human nature, it is abundantly clear, as we have seen, that man's moral capacity, his capacity for self-improvement, is, according to Green, the result of a spiritual force, external to man, gradually reproducing itself in him, and not the product of his own internal system. That utilitarianism leads, therefore, as indicated in (v), to a justification of the status quo, to a legitimization of what is, that it robs man of the desire for self-improvement in the sense Green intended and in fact recognizes no such concept of self-improvement, is undeniable. However, this is a problem not of the internal consistency of utilitarianism but of the imperatives of the market system and the nature of market man.[40]

A similar failure to evaluate adequately the utilitarian argument may be discerned in his other criticisms. Thus, Green's argument (ii) really skirts the issue, for the primary element in the liberal analysis of man and society was always the accumulation, not of pleasures, but of the material means to acquire pleasures. The concept of man as an infinite consumer of utilities, as Macpherson has noted, was merely more

---

40 The argument in this paragraph is based on C.B. Macpherson's discussion of obligation in Hobbes. See *The Political Theory of Possessive Individualism: Hobbes to Locke* (Oxford: at the Clarendon Press, 1962), Chap. 2, sec. 4.

My remarks should not be taken as suggesting that one cannot be both a devout theist and a utilitarian; Hobbes, for example, was both. It was not Green's theology that prevented him from accepting the arguments of utilitarianism but his abhorrence of a morality determined by the dictates of the market.

readily acceptable and less offensive than the concept of man as an infinite appropriator, which, however, was the essential concept for the justification of the capitalist market economy.[41] Furthermore, the means to the acquisition of pleasures, as
distinct from pleasures themselves, can obviously be accumulated, and whereas
their accumulation in great numbers would undoubtedly constitute a pleasant state
of existence, as indicated in (vi), they could nonetheless be quantified in clearly
definable terms.

Green's contention in (iv) that pleasures cannot logically be conceived as determining desire (since this would amount to putting the cart before the horse) does
not speak to the real issue raised by his disagreement with the utilitarian argument:
the radically different views of human nature underlying the two ethical systems.
The individual's desire for self-satisfaction through the attainment of pleasure
stems, according to the utilitarian view, from his nature, and he requires no prior
experience of pleasure to desire it, although experience may teach him that a certain
course of action will yield greater pleasure than another. Thus, Green is in effect
talking past the utilitarian: he presents a counter-concept of man, arguing persua-
sively on its behalf, but at no time does he come to terms with the utilitarian model
of man or its social basis.

Finally, in (vii) Green is clearly mistaken. Equality is certainly not an element of
the end of utilitarianism; on the contrary, inequality must characterize the capitalist
market in order to keep it functioning, and Green, interestingly enough, does not
contest this provision since he too, as we have seen, accepts the inequality of property as an inescapable fact. However, equality is, just as certainly, a necessary
component of the utilitarian analysis, for it is a basic premise of this analysis that
individuals are by nature both equally capable and desirous of pleasure and equally
able to shift for themselves in the market. Indeed, as has already been pointed out, it
is only upon an assumption of equality that the market system can be vindicated.

Green's critique of utilitarianism on these grounds is therefore a rejection, not
merely of utilitarian ethics, but of market morality itself. This rejection was
observed in the last chapter in Green's condemnation of man's animal nature – his
selfish, competitive, pleasure-seeking nature. He took issue with the philosophy that
erected this nature as the highest level of human achievement. But Green failed to
appreciate the social nature of this philosophy: utilitarianism was a valid philosophical system precisely because it accurately portrayed bourgeois man and bourgeois
society. It is bourgeois man who is capable of no higher morality than market morality, who is an insatiable consumer and appropriator of utilities, a rational calculator
of pleasures and pains, and who must be assumed equal on some basic level with

41 C.B. Macpherson, *Democratic Theory: Essays in Retrieval* (Oxford: at the Clarendon Press,
1973), pp. 29-30

other men if market morality is to be justifiable. And it is bourgeois society that best fulfils this nature. In the final analysis, Green saw utilitarianism as internally inconsistent because he perceived man as essentially unlike the way he was depicted by the liberal tradition, and he perceived this difference, as I have argued, because the changing social conditions of human existence had demanded a fundamental transformation in the way men saw each other and themselves. What bothered Green about the utilitarian system (although he himself was not aware of it) was not its lack of internal consistency – for, if he had fully comprehended it, it would not have appeared to him to be self-contradictory – but the market assumptions on which it is based and the society it seeks to justify.

At the same time, Green's inability to appreciate the historical nature and limitations of utilitarianism is ultimately a result of the self-contradictory nature of his own thought. He fully accepted and defended as universal and necessary the major institutions of the capitalist market system, including freedom of contract, the right of unlimited individual appropriation, and the alienation of labour. His rejection of utilitarianism, therefore, was based not upon that theory's support of such institutions, but rather on its conception of man as an egoistic, infinite desirer of pleasures. It was his failure to see the necessary connection between the market nature of man and capitalism, his view of this system and of the nature of man as a mere desirer of pleasure as essentially independent – a view we have seen to be historically unfounded – that blinded him to the social nature of utilitarianism as the justificatory theory of market society.

8

Conclusion

The social and political thought of T.H. Green constitutes on one hand a profound break with the classical liberal tradition and on the other hand a firm justification of its most essential tenets. Green argues, we have seen, that the ultimate end of man is to be found, not in the selfish pursuit of pleasure or material well-being, but in the active, creative exercise and fulfilment of his powers and capacities. This, he maintains, is the true end of human endeavour because it alone is adequate to the real nature of man as a reproduction of the eternal consciousness. The realization of human possibilities is, moreover, conceived of by Green as an end that is both non-exclusive and non-competitive – a common good which, in being achieved by individuals, represents their greatest possible contribution to the general good. It is, finally, a good in which all persons partake as ends in themselves, and not merely as means to the selfish ends of others.

At the same time Green's work serves to rationalize and legitimize the rights and institutions of capitalist market society. Appropriation, in his view, is a function of man's higher nature, necessary to provide him with the permanent instruments of self-satisfaction and self-expression. His nature as a self-determining actor requires that free play be given to all his powers in order that they might be fully developed. Accordingly, individuals must be granted the right of unlimited private appropriation. Although some of the freedoms of the market, the freedoms of trade and bequest, give rise to inequalities, they must be protected, for interference with them would impinge upon the free exercise of individual powers and hence impede the realization of the true good. Furthermore, Green's argument continues, the free market system is constantly redressing the balance by creating new wealth and distributing it to all sectors of society. In addition, there will in any event be inequality as a result of the diversity of human talents. The true good, the perfecting of man, presupposes, in short, the capitalist market system as a condition of its actualization. The end of the state, therefore, is simply to guarantee such rights and such secure and stable conditions as are necessary to ensure the smooth and efficient operation of that system.

Green's assurances notwithstanding, there is in fact an unresolvable incompatibility between the capitalist market system and the possible realization of the true good. The right of unlimited individual appropriation leads inexorably to the permanent division of society into two classes: the property-owning and the propertyless. This condition effectively disqualifies the latter from developing themselves because it excludes them from free access to the means of labour, the means of self-satisfaction and self-expression. Simply to survive they must sell their labour in order to gain access to the instruments of production. This results, therefore, not in the full development of their powers, but in the transfer of some of their powers to the owners of property for their use and enjoyment. There cannot, then, be that equal, non-competitive, and non-exclusive development of persons Green envisaged. On the contrary, the complete exercise of the market freedoms he allows produces instead a continuous net transfer of powers from the non-property-owning class to the propertied class and the virtual exclusion of the former from any participation in the true good.

This contradiction in Green has been attributed to a conflict between two inconsistent ontologies underlying the liberal-democratic tradition: the concept of man as an exerter and enjoyer of his capacities versus the concept of man as an infinite consumer and appropriator of utilities – the former implied by Green's theory of self-realization, the latter by his justification of capitalist market society. I have suggested that this inconsistency is ultimately reducible to Green's self-contradictory theory of human nature as consisting in two antagonistic, yet coexisting, parts: a selfish, appetitive aspect and a social, creative aspect. Although these two natures as described by Green do not correspond perfectly to the two ontologies – appropriation is conceived of as a function of man's higher nature rather than of his lower, appetitive self – I have maintained that this is the consequence of Green's failure to assess adequately the social foundations of the two aspects of his model. An additional result of this inadequate assessment is the inconsistency between Green's rejection of market behaviour and morality, as indicated by his disapproval of the lower nature of man, as well as his critique of utilitarian ethics and his defence of the market system. In the final analysis, I have argued, Green's dichotomous theory of human nature is a faithful representation of man in advanced, industrialized market society, reflecting his alienated condition – the tension between his actual appetitive and appropriative existence and his real creative and self-developing nature, rendered possible by the newly liberated human and technological forces of production.

Furthermore, I have argued that, although Green was fully aware of the class-divided nature of his society, he failed to perceive its true basis in the capitalist market economy that dominated nineteenth-century England. This economy results in a division of society into the owners of capital and the dispossessed. Had Green appreciated this relation, he would logically have had to condemn the market system. In the event, he traced the class structure of his society to the conquest of the land and the control of government by a class of feudal landlords. This had led to the legitimization of rights of property, inconsistent with its idea, which had further exacerbated the inequalities of wealth and thus created a population of serfs, their forcible eviction from the land, and eventually their 'agglomeration' in the centres of mining and manufacture. This, he contended, was the origin of the proletariat and the great inequities of property. The continued poverty and misery of the members of the labouring class was thus the result of their debased, degraded, and demoralized condition, the mentality of serfdom. Their inability to better themselves, Green held, stemmed not from any obstacles inherent in the market system but from the underdeveloped state of their consciousness.

The classes of his society were perceived by Green as determined by differences in the shared consciousness of their members, in the relative predominance of the animal or spiritual aspects of man. On the lower end of this sliding scale of human nature is the proletarian, whose personality is dominated by selfish desires to satisfy animal appetites; who has little or no notion of self as surviving the satisfaction of these wants, no adequate consciousness of his real or possible self, thus little or no capacity for independence or self-determination, and no conception of the desirability or efficacy of appropriation as a means of self-realization; and who, finally – because Green saw appropriation as a barometer of rationality – is relatively less rational than the members of other social classes. At the top of this scale was the capitalist, having a strong social nature and the desire to contribute to the general well-being through his own self-perfection; a well-defined, fairly accurate concept of his possible self, i.e. true self-consciousness; and a fully rational capacity for self-determination through the full, free exercise of the rights afforded him by society, including the right of unlimited acquisition and full participation in the market. Somewhere between these two extremes lay the feudal landlord who on one hand has shown his independence and rationality by his appropriations yet on the other hand exercises his rights in a highly selfish manner and with little contribution to the well-being of society as a whole.

Green's ideal society is one in which class differences have disappeared, not those inequalities of wealth that follow inevitably from the diversity of human capacities and vocations, but the differences of consciousness that he deemed the most significant divisive force in society, the cause of class conflict. This ideal was the basis of his program of legislative reform, his support of factory, health, and housing legislation, and his proposals for land and temperance legislation and reform of the educational and political systems. Green saw the capitalist class as the universal class, representing and embodying the interests and aspirations of humanity as a whole. He hoped his reforms would create conditions that would allow the 'bourgeoisification' of all persons: the feudal nobility, by encouraging the employment of capitalist methods of production on the land and undermining their political power; the proletariat, by alleviating the wretched, debilitating conditions of its existence and, more important, by educating its members to enable them to moralize themselves and 'raise' their own consciousness.

In this instance as well, however, Green failed to see the essential inconsistency of his position. A capitalist class cannot be a universal class; its very existence implies the existence of a dispossessed class. A society dominated by a capitalist market economy cannot be classless; its smooth and efficient operation generates a division of society into owners and non-owners of capital. Ultimately therefore, as elsewhere, Green's error resulted from his failure to comprehend the historical foundations of the two natures of man he postulated and to appreciate the true conditions of the existence of the market system.

Finally, Green's ascription of man's dichotomous nature not to social forces but to the immutable circumstances of his life – the ascription of his lower self to his sentience and his higher self to the reproduction in him of the eternal mind – led him to perceive this divided, self-contradictory nature as an inescapable condition of human existence. This position reflects an implicit recognition and acceptance of the limitations on human development inevitably imposed by the capitalist system, an acceptance of alienation as an unalterable and unavoidable fact, of the continued domination of man's nature by his selfish appetitive tendencies, by those attributes of human nature which the market system evokes and nurtures and the suppression, if not the outright suffocation, of his nature as an unselfish, social, active, and creative being. Green's system is in the end internally inconsistent: the good society he envisages is ultimately unrealizable within the conditions he sets for its attainment.

2

For a number of reasons contemporary political scientists have tended to minimize the importance of Green's contribution to the history of political thought. His writings are usually painfully difficult. Their scarcity compared to the abundant output of some of the luminaries of the nineteenth century, especially Mill and Marx, has almost certainly led to a devaluation of Green's significance. In addition, Green spoke to an age and to issues that often seem to have long lost their relevance; the western world has come a long way since Green lectured to overflowing classrooms about self-realization and the true good.

But the impact of Green's life and work should not be underestimated. On a practical level, he supported many reforms that in his lifetime were considered quite radical. His ideas helped to shape the programs, as well as some of the leading personalities,[1] of the Liberal Party. Green's principles and spirit can be clearly discerned in the social legislation passed by the Liberal governments of 1906 to 1916, which laid the foundations of the modern welfare state.

On a theoretical level, Green's influence has been felt well into the twentieth century.[2] The notion of man as essentially an exerter and developer of his capacities and of his true good as lying in his self-perfection, the realization of his possible self, although neither unique nor original in Green, was given an important impetus in western political theory by his work, and served to animate liberal-democratic thought for some time after his death. Although we have more recently witnessed, in the work of the modern liberal empiricists, a return to concepts that predate Green, our thought and our ideals continue to reflect the force of his ideas. Green is unquestionably one of the major architects of the modern vocabulary of social and political values.

Many of the ideas advanced by Green can be found in a less developed form in the work of John Stuart Mill. Indeed, despite the obvious differences between the two theorists in terms of the traditions upon which they built, the similarity of their thought has generally been recognized.[3] Green's moral philosophy, however, is in

---

1 Most notably, Herbert Asquith, British prime minister, 1908-16, and James Bryce and R.B. Haldane, cabinet members during this period. Although 'I never "worshipped at the Temple's inner shrine,"' Asquith writes, 'I owe more than I can say to Green's gymnastics, both intellectual and moral.' *Memories and Reflections: 1852-1927* (Boston: Little, Brown, 1928), I, p. 24. Cf. his *Studies and Sketches*, 2nd ed. (London: Hutchinson, 1924), p. 22. Speaking of the atmosphere in the country and in the Liberal Party in 1906 that led to the adoption of reform measures, Haldane writes: 'The teaching of men like Thomas Hill Green was penetrating deeply, and that [teaching] turned on much more than *laissez-faire*. There was earnestness about State intervention to be seen everywhere.' *An Autobiography* (Garden City, NY: Doubleday, Doran, 1929), p. 229. For Bryce's evaluation of Green see his 'Professor T.H. Green: In Memoriam,' (*Contemporary Review*, XLI, May 1882) and a slightly modified version of this piece in *Studies in Contemporary Biography* (London: Macmillan, 1903), Chap. 3.

2 The works of such individuals as Ernest Barker, Bernard Bosanquet, A.C. and F.H. Bradley, Edward Caird, A.D. Lindsay, J.H. Muirhead, R.L. Nettleship, David Ritchie, Arnold Toynbee, and William Wallace all bear the stamp of Green's system.

3 Thus, David Ritchie writes: 'There is no reason why the Idealist, after making clear his objections to Hedonism, should not join hands with the Utilitarian. In fact, an ethical system like Green's is really, on its practical side, J.S. Mill's Utilitarianism with a securer basis and a criterion provided, which Mill cannot logically provide, for distinguishing the different *qualities* of pleasure' (*The Principles of State Interference*, London, 1896, p. 145). See also Melvin Richter, *The Politics of Conscience* (London: Weidenfeld and Nicolson, 1964) pp. 204, 263. The depth of the similarity between the two theorists, however, has not been fully appreciated. See Appendix.

many ways more penetrating than Mill's, and the ideas of self-development and of the dual nature of man are more throroughly and more clearly articulated. By the same token, the contradictions and inconsistencies are more emphasized, more readily discernible, in Green's work. This may be explained both by the somewhat later perspective with which Green wrote as well as the fact that, unlike Mill, he felt no sense of loyalty to, and was thus not restrained by, the utilitarian tradition.

At the same time, Green's work reflects many of the same concerns that preoccupied Marx. Green's system represents the reaction of liberal thought to the morally reprehensible living conditions of the majority of English people and is an attempt to lay the philosophical groundwork for measures that would substantially improve their lot, to redefine the ends of western civilization in more human and humane terms. The philosophical systems of Green and Marx both express the realities of nineteenth-century industrial-capitalist market society: the increasing division of society, the growing misery and deprivation of the proletariat, the new possibilities unfolding for man as a result of his achievements in industry and technology, and his deepening alienation. Even Green's ideal of the just society as a classless society in which individuals are enjoyers and exerters of their capacities, self-realizers who are ends in themselves, bears a striking resemblance to the Marxist vision – with one telling difference: Green was so convinced of the necessity and intrinsic justice of the market system that this system set the limits within which he perceived the problems of his society and beyond which he did not venture in attempting to formulate a solution.

Green was able to inject a new democratic dimension into the mainstream of liberal thought: first, in his effort to transcend market morality through his notion of the true good as consisting in full and equal human development; second, in his conception of the good society as a classless society. However, he held fast to the belief, not merely that capitalism forms no serious impediment to the actualization of his democratic ideal, but also that it is a condition of its attainment. This belief rendered his analysis inherently short-sighted and his vision ultimately self-defeating.

Notes towards a comparison of Green and J.S. Mill

Students of Green and Mill have generally granted that, notwithstanding the obvious differences between their work arising from the different philosophical foundations upon which they constructed their systems, there is a large area of agreement between the two nineteenth-century theorists. Little attempt has been made, however, to define the extent of this similarity. A thorough discussion of Mill's thought, such as would be required by a full treatment of its resemblance to Green's work, is of course not possible here. Nevertheless, it is both possible and important to outline some of the chief elements of his thought and compare them with Green's system.

This exercise will also shed light on the limitations of Green's critique of Mill. There can be no serious quarrel with Green's general argument that Mill's moral philosophy does not follow from his utilitarian principles. However, his explanation of this inconsistency, though perhaps acceptable on a superficial level, is hardly a satisfactory resolution of the problem. Here, as in his critique of utilitarianism, Green passes over the more significant issues. I suggest that the inconsistency he perceived is symptomatic of a much more profound contradiction because it parallels directly an inconsistency we have already noticed in his own thought.

Mill's acceptance of the major assumptions of utilitarianism, including, as Green pointed out, the notion that pleasure is the sole object of desire, implies acceptance of the Hobbes-to-Bentham concept of man as a self-moving mechanism, an infinite consumer and appropriator of utilities. This view is further substantiated by Mill's justification of the major institutions of capitalist market society. On the other hand, Mill's attempt, much like Green's own, to transcend the morality of the market by differentiating between higher and lower pleasures and his conviction that man could improve his character imply a rejection of the liberal model of man and the espousal of a concept of man as more than a creature of appetites, i.e. as an exerter and developer of his capacities. These two concepts of human nature are, however, incompatible; the fulfilment of the one implies the negation of the other. This, I submit, is the basis of the inconsistency in Mill's thought, but as in Green's it may be traced to a self-contradictory model of human nature. Indeed, the similarity between the two philosophers' theories of human nature, as well as their theories of social classes, is striking.

Though distinguishing between lower and higher pleasures, Mill perceives this variation in much the same way as Green views the wants of man, that is, as expressions of either a lower or higher, an animal or a spiritual, nature. 'The comparison of the Epicurean life to that of beasts' Mill writes 'is felt as degrading, precisely because a beast's pleasures do not satisfy a human being's conceptions of happiness. Human beings have faculties more elevated than the animal appetites, and when once made conscious of them, do not regard anything as happiness which does not include their gratification.'[1] Similarly, claiming the support of those who have experienced both types of pleasures, he argues that 'their feelings and judgment declare the pleasures derived from the higher faculties to be preferable *in kind*, apart from the question of intensity, to those of which the animal nature, disjoined from the higher faculties, is susceptible.'[2]

It is within this framework that Mill's concept of 'the improvement of mankind'[3] must be understood. Thus, in criticizing Bentham's theory of human nature, he writes: 'Man is never recognized by him as a being capable of pursuing *spiritual* perfection as an end; of desiring, for its own sake, the conformity of his own character to his standard of excellence, without hope of good, or fear of evil, from other source than his own inward consciousness.'[4] It is therefore the moralization of man, in the same sense as urged by Green, i.e. the accession of his better self, the gradual subordination of his animal inclinations, that Mill intends by his references to man's 'spiritual development,' 'the cultivation of his higher nature.'[5] This too is the basis of his favourable discussion of von Humboldt, and his agreement with the latter's statement that 'the end of man, or that which is prescribed by the eternal or immutable dictates of reason, and not suggested by vague and transient desires, is the highest and most harmonious *development of his powers* to a complete and consistent whole.'[6] The end of man, in Mill's view, is to be found in his 'self-development,' the development and cultivation of his capacities. 'Among the works of man, which

---

1 *Utilitarianism*, in *Collected Works of John Stuart Mill*, X, ed. by J.M. Robson (Toronto: University of Toronto Press, 1969), pp. 210-11

2 Ibid., p. 213. Cf. pp. 212-3; *On Liberty*, in *Collected Works of John Stuart Mill*, XVIII, ed. by J.M. Robson (Toronto: University of Toronto Press, 1977), p. 278; and *Principles of Political Economy*, in *Collected Works of John Stuart Mill*, II and III, ed. by J.M. Robson (Toronto: University of Toronto Press, 1965), III, p. 768

3 *Autobiography of John Stuart Mill* (New York: Columbia University Press), p. 100

4 'Bentham,' in *Collected Works*, X, p. 95; emphasis added. Cf. pp. 95-6, 97-8.

5 *On Liberty*, p. 270

6 Quoted by Mill, *On Liberty*, p. 261; emphasis added. Cf. pp. 261-2, 274; and *Autobiography*, p. 179.

human life is rightly employed in perfecting and beautifying,' he asserts, 'the first in importance is surely man himself ... Human nature is not a machine to be built after a model, and set to do exactly the work prescribed for it, but a tree, which requires to grow and develop itself on all sides, according to the tendency of the inward forces which make it a living thing.'[7]

A significant feature of Mill's concept of self-perfection is individuality. He maintains in fact that 'individuality is the same thing with development, and that it is only the cultivation of individuality which produces, or can produce, well-developed human beings.'[8] Similarly, he speaks of 'the importance, to man and society, of a large variety in types of character, and of giving full freedom to human nature to expand itself in innumerable and conflicting directions.'[9]

This position was not a justification of human selfishness. On the contrary, Mill depicts such tendencies in man as undesirable and encourages 'the better development of the social part of his nature, rendered possible by the restraint put upon the selfish part'[10]; he argues that there is no 'inherent necessity that any human being should be a selfish egotist, devoid of every feeling or care but those which centre in his own miserable individuality.'[11] Human history is the history of the gradual strengthening of the natural 'social feelings of mankind.'[12] 'In an *improving* state of the human mind, the influences are constantly on the increase, which tend to generate in each individual a feeling of unity with all the rest; which feeling, if perfect, would make him never think of, or desire, any beneficial condition for himself, in the benefits of which they are not included.'[13]

Mill's concept of man is of a being composed of two parts or tendencies: a selfish, appetitive aspect and a social, creative aspect. Furthermore, for him the true good, the ultimate end of all human endeavour, is the perfection of human powers and capacities – the development and satisfaction of his higher nature and the suppression of his animal appetites. It is a common good, which, in being achieved by each, is a contribution to all, and which cannot be attained by one at the expense of others. 'In proportion to the development of his individuality,' Mill maintains, 'each person becomes more valuable to others. There is a greater fulness of life about his own existence, and when there is more life in the units there is more in the mass which is composed of them.'[14]

7 *On Liberty*, p. 263; cf. pp. 265-6.
8 Ibid., p. 267; cf. pp. 274-5.
9 *Autobiography*, p. 177; cf. *On Liberty*, pp. 226, 261.
10 *On Liberty*, p. 266
11 *Utilitarianism*, p. 216; cf. *On Liberty*, p. 279.
12 *Utilitarianism*, p. 231
13 *Utilitarianism*, p. 232; emphasis added. Cf. *Principles of Political Economy*, II, p. 210; and *Autobiography*, p. 163.
14 *On Liberty*, p. 266

In the comparatively early state of human advancement in which we now live, a person cannot indeed feel that entireness of sympathy with all others, which would make any real discordance in the general direction of their conduct in life impossible; but already a person in whom the social feeling is at all developed, cannot bring himself to think of the rest of his fellow-creatures as struggling rivals with him for the means of happiness, whom he must desire to see defeated in their object in order that he may succeed in his. The deeply rooted conception which every individual even now has of himself as a social being, tends to make him feel it one of his natural wants that there should be harmony between his feelings and aims and those of his fellow-creatures.[15]

Unlike Green, Mill is not an opponent of all competition. To be sure, he decries some of 'the inevitable fruits of immense competition,' its tendencies to efface human individuality and to commercialize, and hence cheapen, the arts, thereby reducing their effectiveness as an instrument of moral improvement.[16] 'But if competition has its evils,' he writes, 'it prevents greater evils.'[17] Competition, in Mill's estimation, is indispensable, not only for industrial progress, but to achieve as well 'that multiform development of human nature, those manifold unlikenesses, that diversity of tastes and talents, and variety of intellectual points of view, which not only form a great part of the interest of human life, but by bringing intellects into stimulating collision ... are the mainspring of mental and moral progression.'[18] In short, competition, by contributing to individual self-development, contributes to the good of all. Indeed, he points to indications that the intensity of competition is diminishing, suggesting that this will reduce its unfavourable features. 'Competition will be as active as ever,' he predicts, 'but the number of competitors will be brought within manageable bounds.'[19]

One of the chief obstacles to the realization of a common good, according to Mill, is the division of society into classes. All classes, he believes, are concerned primarily with the interests of their own members, a situation which renders unified activity toward a shared good virtually impossible. He argues that granting outright political power to any one class would result in class rule in the interest of the dominant class and be contrary to the well-being of society at large.[20] It is for this reason that he ultimately opposes majority rule in England:

15 *Utilitarianism*, p. 233. Cf. pp. 218, 231-2; and *Autobiography*, p. 100.
16 'Civilization,' in *Collected Works*, XVIII, pp. 132-5
17 *Principles of Political Economy*, III, p. 795
18 Ibid., II, p. 209; cf. III, pp. 794-6.
19 'Civilization,' p. 136
20 J.E. Broadbent, 'The Importance of Class in the Political Theory of John Stuart Mill,' *Canadian Journal of Political Science*, I: No. 3 (Sept. 1968), pp. 277-9

The numerical majority of any society whatever, must consist of persons all standing in the same social position, and having, in the main, the same pursuits; namely, unskilled manual labourers. And we mean no disparagement to them: whatever we say to their disadvantage, we say equally of a numerical majority of shopkeepers or of squires. Where there is identity of position and pursuits, there also will be identity of partialities, passions, and prejudices; and to give any one set of partialities, passions, and prejudices, absolute power, without counterbalance from partialities, passions, and prejudices of a different sort, is the way to render the correction of any of those imperfections hopeless; to make one narrow, mean type of human nature universal and perpetual; and to crush every influence which tends to the further improvement of man's intellectual and moral nature.[21]

While all classes are similar in so far as they are selfish, they represent, Mill contends, 'varieties of human nature.'[22] Of the nobility he is in general quite critical, remarking upon their particularly selfish attitudes. 'All privileged and powerful classes, as such,' he writes, 'have used their power in the interest of their own selfishness, and have indulged their self-importance in despising ... those who were, in their estimation, degraded, by being under the necessity of working for their benefit.'[23] At the same time he views the use and control of land in England by the aristocracy as inimical to the general economic well-being. His recommendations for the curtailment of the rights of inheritance and property in land, though not radical enough to have any far-reaching effects, are, like Green's proposals, aimed at encouraging the application of capitalist methods in the use of the soil and at transforming the aristocracy into a capitalist class.[24]

In Mill's comparison of the classes of his society, the working class occupies the lowest position. It is in the very nature of the labourer's daily existence, Mill suggests, that this be so: his 'employment is a routine' and his 'way of life brings him in contact with no variety of impressions, circumstances, or ideas.'[25] 'An employer of labour' he maintains 'is on the average more intelligent than a labourer; for he must

---

21 'Bentham,' p. 107. Mill goes on in this paragraph to refer to majority rule 'not as being just in itself but as being less unjust than any other footing on which the matter can be placed.' Later, of course, Mill abandoned one-man-one-vote democracy as an immediate possibility. See *Considerations on Representative Government*, in *Collected Works of John Stuart Mill*, XIX, ed. by J.M. Robson (Toronto: University of Toronto Press, 1977), chaps 7, 8; and 'Thoughts on Parliamentary Reform,' ibid., pp. 322-5.
22 'De Tocqueville on Democracy in America [II],' in *Collected Works*, XVIII, p. 196
23 *Principles of Political Economy*, III, p. 760. Cf. 'De Tocqueville on Democracy in America [I],' in *Collected Works*, XVIII, p. 78; and *Autobiography*, p. 120.
24 *Principles of Political Economy*, Book 2, chap. 2; cf. 'Coleridge,' in *Collected Works*, X, pp. 157-8.
25 *Representative Government*, p. 469

labour with his head, and not solely with his hands.'[26] Furthermore, he argues, though a class of '*prolétaires* ... in abject poverty, like the greatest part of our rural population, or which expends its surplus earnings in gin or in waste, be kept in political subjection,' they are also dangerous, because they are capable of political violence.[27]

Workers are not able to look after their own interests; they must be taught 'the virtues of independence.'[28] Mill, unlike Green, adds his voice to the proponents of the Poor Law legislation of 1834:

If the condition of a person receiving relief is made as eligible as that of the labourer who supports himself by his own exertions, the system strikes at the root of all individual industry and self-government; and, if fully acted up to, would require as its supplement an organized system of compulsion, for governing and setting to work like cattle, those who had been removed from the influence of the motives that act on human beings. But if, consistently with guaranteeing all persons against absolute want, the condition of those who are supported by legal charity can be kept considerably less desirable than the condition of those who find support for themselves, none but beneficial consequences can arise from a law which renders it impossible for any person, except by his own choice, to die from insufficiency of food. That in England at least this supposition can be realized, is proved by the experience of a long period preceding the close of the last century, as well as by that of many highly pauperized districts in more recent times, which have been dispauperized by adopting strict rules of poor law administration, to the great and permanent benefit of the whole labouring class.[29]

Mill discusses three ways besides legislation affecting landed property by which the moral and economic conditions of the labouring class might be improved: education, political participation, and the co-operative movement in industry.

By far the worst disability of the members of the working class is for Mill their lack of education, which he considers a measure not only of their low intellectual level but of their low moral level as well, that is, their incapacity for desiring higher objects, for living for an end other than the satisfaction of their selfish, animal wants. 'The prospect of the future' he warns 'depends on the degree in which they can be made rational beings.'[30] Referring to the need for an educational qualification for voting, he asserts:

26 Ibid., p. 475. Cf. pp. 411-2; 'De Tocqueville on Democracy in America [II],' p. 169; and *Utilitarianism*, p. 213.
27 'De Tocqueville on Democracy in America [II],' p. 166
28 *Principles of Political Economy*, III, p. 763
29 Ibid., pp. 961-2. Mill also argues that those who receive charity should not have the vote because they lack independence (*Representative Government*, p. 472).
30 *Principles of Political Economy*, III, p. 763

None are so illiberal, none so bigoted in their hostility to improvement, none so superstitiously attached to the stupidest and worst of old forms and usages, as the uneducated. None are so unscrupulous, none so eager to clutch at whatever they have not and others have, as the uneducated in possession of power. An uneducated mind is almost incapable of clearly conceiving the rights of others. There is a great abatement in the dread which people of property once entertained of universal suffrage ... But, whatever be the most provable complexion of the evil to be feared, no lover of improvement can desire that the *predominant* power should be turned over to persons in the mental and moral condition of the English working classes.[31]

Earlier in the same essay he comments:

If it is asserted that all persons ought to be equal in every description of right recognized by society, I answer, not until all are equal in worth as human beings. It is the fact, that one person is *not* as good as another ... Putting aside for the present the consideration of moral worth, of which, though more important even than intellectual, it is not so easy to find an available test; a person who cannot read, is not as good, for the purpose of human life, as one who can.[32]

'Those who most need to be made wiser and better' Mill points out 'usually desire it least, and if they desired it, would be incapable of finding the way to it by their own lights.'[33] The state must accordingly provide the funds to ensure that the children of the working class are educated. Such a system will not aggravate the dependence of the labourers. On the contrary: 'Instruction, when it is really such, does not enervate, but strengthens, as well as enlarges the active faculties: in whatever manner acquired, its effect on the mind is favourable to the spirit of independence: and when, unless had gratuitously, it would not be had at all, help in this form has the opposite tendency to that which in so many other cases makes it objectionable; it is help towards doing without help.'[34] A further product of education that, as we have seen, is an element in the moral progress of man is in Mill's view the fostering of a 'feeling of unity' among men, the development of the social nature.[35] But Mill cautions against state education, which he perceives as a threat to individuality, 'a mere contrivance for moulding people to be exactly like one another.'[36]

31 'Thoughts on Parliamentary Reform,' p. 327
32 Ibid., p. 323
33 *Principles of Political Economy*, III, p. 947
34 Ibid., p. 949. Cf. 'The Claims of Labour,' in *Collected Works of John Stuart Mill*, IV, ed. by J.M. Robson (Toronto: University of Toronto, 1967), pp. 378-9.
35 *Utilitarianism*, p. 226
36 *On Liberty*, p. 302

Second, Mill argues that participation in the political system is itself an educative process. To be sure, he came to consider education as a prerequisite for extending the franchise: 'universal teaching must precede universal enfranchisement.'[37] Nevertheless, he sees the enfranchisement of the people as a factor in their moralization, as tending to broaden their interests and hence to develop their social feelings while suppressing their egoistic tendencies:

Among the foremost benefits of free government is that education of the intelligence and of the sentiments which is carried down to the very lowest ranks of the people when they are called to take a part in acts which directly affect the great interests of their country ... People think it fanciful to expect so much from what seems so slight a cause – to recognize a potent instrument of mental improvement in the exercise of political franchises by manual labourers. Yet unless substantial mental cultivation in the mass of mankind is to be a mere vision, this is the road by which it must come.[38]

Third, Mill sees the association of labourers as helping to improve their condition. In general, he considers co-operation an attribute of civilization. 'There is not a more accurate test of the progress of civilization' he writes 'than the progress of cooperation.' He continues:

All combination is compromise: it is the sacrifice of some portion of individual will for a common purpose. The savage cannot bear to sacrifice, for any purpose, the satisfaction of his individual will. His social cannot even temporarily prevail over his selfish feelings, nor his impulses bend to his inclinations ... As any people approach to the condition of savages or of slaves, so are they incapable of acting in concert.[39]

Thus Mill apparently views co-operation as a function of the gradual subordination of man's selfish animal nature and the gradual development of his higher social tendencies. At the same time, co-operation is something that must be learned:

Now the whole course of advancing civilization is a series of such teaching. The labourer in a rude state of society works singly, or if several are brought to work together by the will of a master, they work side by side, but not in concert; one man digs his piece of ground, another digs a similar piece of ground close by him. In the situation of an ignorant labourer, tilling even his own field with his own hand, and associating with no one except his wife and

---

37 *Representative Government*, p. 470
38 Ibid., pp. 467-8. Cf. pp. 411-12, 469; *On Liberty*, p. 305; 'Thoughts on Parliamentary Reform,' pp. 322-3; 'De Tocqueville on Democracy in America [I],' p. 63; and 'De Tocqueville on Democracy in America [II],' pp. 168-9.
39 'Civilization,' p. 122; cf. *Principles of Political Economy*, III, p. 708.

children, what is there that can teach him to co-operate? The division of employments – the accomplishment by the combined labour of several, of tasks which could not be achieved by any number of persons singly – is the great school of co-operation.[40]

The division of labour therefore accounts for 'the greatest novelty of all,' 'the spirit of combination which has grown up among the working classes.' Benefit societies, 'the more questionable Trades Unions,' but most important the association of labourers in the ownership and management of industrial enterprises, all constitue for Mill an indication of the moral improvement of the labourers, as well as an opportunity for their further self-development.[41] 'A people thus progressively trained to combination by the business of their lives' he contends 'become capable of carrying the same habits into new things.'[42]

On the whole, Mill thinks quite highly of the capitalist class. Although he says little specifically about them, we may infer his general estimation of the employers of labour. First and foremost, his justification of the capitalist mode of production implies his belief that the capitalist class was the one best suited to the needs and conditions of modern society. Its members are more intelligent than labourers because they use their minds in their work. They are economically independent, able to govern themselves and their concerns rationally and hence morally better than the labourers. The nature of their work broadens the scope of their interests. In proportion as they identify with their class, they are selfish; however, in so far as they are able to transcend their class interests, they are best capable of contributing to the well-being of society through the market economy.

Furthermore, as in Green's system, market man represents the model of human nature to which the members of the other classes tend to conform. Through legislation Mill hopes to break up the economic basis of the feudal aristocracy, to increase the use of capitalist methods of production on the land, and to transform the nobility into capitalists themselves. In addition, he intends through political reform to reduce their political power.

These measures would eliminate one of the chief reasons for the 'degraded and miserable' condition of the working class[43]:

The social arrangements of modern Europe commenced from a distribution of property which was the result, not of just partition, or acquisition by industry, but of conquest and violence: and notwithstanding what industry has been doing for many centuries to modify the

---

40 'Civilization,' p. 123
41 Ibid., p. 125; cf. *Principles of Political Economy*, Book 4, Chap. 7, secs 4-6.
42 'Civilization,' p. 124
43 *Principles of Political Economy*, II, p. 208

work of force, the system still retains many and large traces of its origin. The laws of property have never yet conformed to the principles oh which the justification of private property rests. They have made property of things which never ought to be property, and absolute property where only a qualified property ought to exist. They have not held the balance fairly between human beings, but have heaped impediments upon some, to give advantage to others; they have purposely fostered inequalities, and prevented all from starting fair in the race.[44]

By removing such legal obstacles to the 'just' operation of the market system, by educating the labouring class (both in a general and a political sense) to make them better able to act as responsible members of society, and by the growth of the co-operative movement, which would make labourers economically independent, Mill hopes to transform the workers as well into full-fledged capitalists.[45]

Mill's social and political thought is thus very much like Green's. There are differences of emphasis and approach as well as variations in content. Nevertheless, the main lines of argument are remarkably similar. Both philosophers portray human nature as consisting of two incompatible and antagonistic, yet coexisting, sides: a selfish, appetitive aspect and a social, moral, creative aspect. Both theorists justify the institutions of market society and are oblivious to the unresolvable contradiction between the moralization of man, the possibility of his self-realization, and the continued existence of market society. Both therefore condemn man to an alienated and unfulfilled dual existence. Both, finally, view their societies as class-divided, with class differences defined as differences in consciousness, in the relative prominence of one side of human nature over the other, and with the capitalist class as representing a higher level of human development than the other classes.[46]

Moreover, Mill, like Green, perceives the good society as a classless one. He conceives the true good as a common good and the elimination of man's selfish

---

44 Ibid., p. 207

45 A further cause of the condition of the proletariat according to Mill is its high birth rate, which leads to greater competition for employment and lower wages. He apparently believes this to be a further aspect of the underdeveloped consciousness of the working class. 'It appears to me impossible' he writes 'but that the increase of intelligence, of education, and of the love of independence among the working classes, must be attended with a corresponding growth of the good sense which manifests itself in provident habits of conduct, and that population, therefore, will bear a gradually diminishing ratio to capital and employment.' *Principles of Political Economy*, III, p. 765. Cf. p. 709; II, p. 208; and 'The Claims of Labour,' pp. 367-8.

46 Although Mill certainly thought more of the capitalist class than the other classes, he did not think as highly of it as did Green. It is apparent from his ranking of persons for the assignment of votes in his system of multiple voting that Mill considered the better-educated members of society as representing the highest level of human development. (See *Representative Government*, pp. 474-7, 508; and 'Thoughts on Parliamentary Reform,' pp. 324-5.)

tendencies as desirable; and he sees the partition of society into classes as an obstacle to the achievement of this end, a promoter of disunity and narrow class interests. The elimination of class differences is his goal when he speaks of the benefits of co-operation:

It is scarcely possible to rate too highly this material benefit, which yet is as nothing compared with the moral revolution in society that would accompany [co-operation]: the healing of the standing feud between capital and labour; the transformation of human life, from a conflict of classes struggling for opposite interests, to a friendly rivalry in the pursuit of a good common to all; the elevation of the dignity of labour; a new sense of security and independence in the labouring class; and the conversion of each human being's daily occupation into a school of the social sympathies and the practical intelligence.[47]

However, Mill's vision, like Green's, is ultimately unattainable in the circumstances he postulates. He mistakenly sees no necessary connection between capitalism and the lower nature of man. He erroneously attributes the existence of classes and class conflict, not to capitalism itself, but rather, much as Green does, to antecedent circumstances and the relatively more or less developed consciousness of the various classes. Mill is therefore unable to see the necessary contradiction between the continued existence of capitalism and the possibility of a classless society, and between this possibility and the transformation of all persons into capitalists – the idealization and universalization of bourgeois man.

---

47 *Principles of Political Economy*, III, p. 792. Cf. p. 793: 'Eventually, and in perhaps a less remote future than may be supposed, we may, through the co-operative principle, see our way to a change in society, which would combine the freedom and independence of the individual, with the moral, intellectual, and economical advantages of aggregate production; and which, without violence or spoliation, or even any sudden disturbance of existing habits and expectations, would realize, at least in the industrial department, the best aspirations of the democratic spirit, by putting an end to the division of society into the industrious and the idle, and effacing all social distinctions but those fairly earned by personal service and exertions.'

Index

Possessive individualism 5-6, 10
Possible self: *see* Real self.
Post-market man 108; *see also* Human nature.
Powers (human) 24, 27, 97 n. 38, 102; development of, as self-realization 32, 33, 41, 42 n. 45, 43, 45, 49, 56-7, 104, 108-9, 124; economic inequality arising from differences in 77; limited by social reform 97; transfer of 105, 125; true freedom defined as development of 97-100, 104; and rights 56-61, 63, 65, 72; and the state 52, 60; in J.S. Mill 132-3; of appropriation 74-5, 77-8, 84, 88, 104, 124; *see also* Man: as exerter of powers.
Practical reason 29-30; *see also* Reason.
Prichard, H.A. 37 n. 20
Proletariat: creation of 78-80, 85, 105, 108, 126, 139-40; transformation of 4 n. 3, 84-5, 88-9, 90, 96-7, 127, 140; trusting of 82, 94; and alcoholism 91; and formation of benefit-societies 83, 138-9; and freedom 98-9; and Green's theory of classes 80-5, 87, 88, 101, 103-6, 126; and industrial-capitalist market society 129; and property 78-80; and social reform 4, 71, 82-3, 89, 90-9, 126-7, 136-8, 140; and the mentality of serfdom 81; as not seeking property 80; as reckless 4, 79, 84, 136; in J.S. Mill 135-41
Property 71-80, 95 n. 27; common 74, 79; origin of 71-4, 98; and Green's justification of capitalist market society 87; and Green's theory of classes 81, 84-7, 125-6; and inequality 76-7, 104, 122; and political resistance 67; and the proletariat 77-80, 81, 84-5, 126,

139-40; and the state 51; as the means of self-realization 72-3, 104; in J.S. Mill 135, 137; in land 79-80, 126, 135; *see also* Appropriation.

Randall, J.H. 15 n. 12
Rationality 84, 87, 88, 99, 101, 126, 136, 139; *see also* Reason.
Real, the 14, 15, 17
Real self: and Green's theory of classes 81, 84, 88, 126; and Green's theory of human nature 30, 100, 107-8, 125; and self-realization 35, 37, 47-9, 124, 128; *see also* Higher nature.
Reality 14, 15, 17, 24
Realization of human powers: *see* Self-realization.
Reason 73, 132; and appropriation 72; and capitalism 88; and freedom 29; and Green's theory of classes 84, 87, 88; and law 52, 55, 87; and self-realization 29-30, 35-6, 55; and the eternal consciousness 19; and the state 52-3, 87; and will 29-30, 84; *see also* Rationality.
Reform Acts 95, 96
Relations 14-28, 34, 35, 39, 43, 47-8, 58
Religion 6-9, 33, 88 n. 78
Richter, Melvin 6-9, 33, 43 n. 49, 66 n. 78, 83 n. 59
Rights 8, 33, 103 n. 52, 124, 126, 137; defined 56, 57-8; foundation of 56-7, 59 n. 45; natural 58-60, 66 n. 78, 67, 69 n. 87, 87; negative 102; recognition of 50, 56-9, 60, 63, 66, 72-4, 77; tenant- 86; and education 94; and freedom 98, 100 n. 43; and law 50-2, 59; and political reform 95; and political resistance 60-70; and the state 50-2, 54, 57, 59, 60, 70, 125; to life and